M000098014

About this Learning Guide

Shmoop Will Make You a Better Lover*
*of Literature, History, Poetry, Life...

Our lively learning guides are written by experts and educators who want to show your brain a good time. Shmoop writers come primarily from Ph.D. programs at top universities, including Stanford, Harvard, and UC Berkeley.

Want more Shmoop? We cover literature, poetry, bestsellers, music, US history, civics, biographies (and the list keeps growing). Drop by our website to see the latest.

www.shmoop.com

Table of Contents

Introduction 4
   In a Nutshell 4
   Why Should I Care? 4
Summary 4
   Book Summary 4
   Scene One 5
   Scene Two 6
   Scene Three 6
   Scene Four 7
   Scene Five 7
   Scene Six 8
   Scene Seven 9
Themes 10
   Theme of Freedom and Confinement 10
   Questions About Freedom and Confinement 10
   Chew on Freedom and Confinement 10
   Theme of Duty 10
   Questions About Duty 11
   Chew on Duty 11
   Theme of Family 11
   Questions About Family 11
   Chew on Family 12
   Theme of Memory and the Past 12
   Questions About Memory and the Past 12
   Chew on Memory and the Past 12
   Theme of Weakness 12
   Questions About Weakness 13
   Chew on Weakness 13
   Theme of Deception and Lies 13
   Questions About Deception and Lies 13
   Chew on Deception and Lies 13
   Theme of Dreams, Hopes, and Plans 14
   Questions About Dreams, Hopes, and Plans 14
   Chew on Dreams, Hopes, and Plans 14
   Theme of Abandonment 14
   Questions About Abandonment 14
   Chew on Abandonment 15
   Theme of Marriage 15
   Questions About Marriage 15
   Chew on Marriage 15
   Theme of Gender 15
   Questions About Gender 15
   Chew on Gender 16

Theme of Love 16
Questions About Love 16
Chew on Love 16
Theme of Drugs and Alcohol 16
Questions About Drugs and Alcohol 17
Chew on Drugs and Alcohol 17
Quotes 17
Freedom and Confinement Quotes 17
Duty Quotes 22
Family Quotes 26
Memory and the Past Quotes 33
Weakness Quotes 38
Deception and Lies Quotes 45
Dreams, Hopes, and Plans Quotes 49
Abandonment Quotes 52
Marriage Quotes 55
Gender Quotes 59
Love Quotes 62
Drugs and Alcohol Quotes 65
Plot Analysis 67
Classic Plot Analysis 67
Booker's Seven Basic Plots Analysis: Tragedy 68
Three Act Plot Analysis 68
Study Questions 69
Characters 69
All Characters 69
Laura Wingfield Character Analysis 69
Laura Wingfield Timeline and Summary 70
Tom Wingfield Character Analysis 71
Tom Wingfield Timeline and Summary 71
Amanda Wingfield Character Analysis 72
Amanda Wingfield Timeline and Summary 73
Jim O'Connor Character Analysis 73
Jim O'Connor Timeline and Summary 74
Character Roles 74
Character Clues 75
Literary Devices 76
Symbols, Imagery, Allegory 76
Setting 77
Narrator Point of View 78
Genre 78
Tone 78
Writing Style 79
What's Up With the Title? 79
What's Up With the Epigraph? 79
Did You Know? 79
Trivia 79

Steaminess Rating 80
Allusions and Cultural References 80
Best of the Web 80
Movie or TV Productions 80
Images 81
Documents 81

Introduction

In a Nutshell

The Glass Menagerie is a play first produced in 1944. The author, <u>Tennessee Williams</u>, was launched into fame and made victim to the forties' equivalent of literary paparazzi because of it. The play revolves around a young man begrudgingly supporting the family his father has abandoned. It also features a painfully shy and slightly crippled sister character, whose preoccupation with a collection of glass animals draws her away from reality. Set against the backdrop of the <u>Depression</u>, the family struggles together with the past, the future, and one another.

Why Should I Care?

OK, so you never lived in the <u>Great Depression</u>. We didn't either. Or abandoned your family for Jolly-Roger-style adventure. But have you ever called your mother a mean name in the heat of the moment? Or tried to live your own personal life but gotten hassled about it?

So you can totally appreciate Tom's situation. We mean, the guy is twenty-one and stuck in a little apartment with a mother who won't let him drink and a sister who is desperately single. Can you imagine trying to juggle all that? Toss in dreams of being a writer, the fact that your father abandoned you, and a boring job in a shoe warehouse. The point is, things suck for Tom. But at the same time, he really has an obligation – the family will completely suffer without him. Pretty compelling, if you ask us.

Summary

Book Summary

The play begins with a current-day (1940s at the time) Tom explaining to us that the play is his memory (1930s) being re-told, and has lots of funky memory elements in it like weird lighting and music. We are also introduced to a large screen that Williams uses to project images and pictures on as the play progresses. Tom explains that his father happily abandoned them years ago. We see Tom having dinner with his mother, Amanda, and his sister Laura. Amanda expresses a desire for Laura to have "gentlemen callers" (a.k.a. dates) as she used to, back when she was a Southern Belle.

Laura describes a boy named Jim she used to have a thing for in high school, and we see her glass menagerie obsession. Amanda gets angry at Laura for dropping out of a typing class due to her painfully shy nature.

The conflict with Tom is quickly established; he is at odds with his mother because he hates his job and wants to leave, but has a duty to support the family. His mother calls him selfish for his

constant reading, dancing, drinking, and escaping to the movies. Laura encourages them to make up, which they do – ostensibly. But the issue is unresolved.

Amanda asks Tom to get a gentleman caller for his sister, which he does – one of his friend's from work that turns out to be the Jim that Laura had spoken of. Amanda gets all excited and prepares the house. When Laura finds out that it's Jim coming to visit, she hides in the living room. Jim, however, talks to her and gets her to open up. They bond; they kiss; Jim is engaged to someone else. He takes off, Laura gets sad, and Amanda yells at her son and then comforts Laura during Tom's closing speech to the audience. Tom reveals to us that he abandoned his family shortly after that night, but has been haunted by Laura, the sister he abandoned, ever since.

Scene One

- OK, the scenery first. You've got your standard mid- Depression apartment complete with fire escape and desperation, some fuzzy lighting which Williams claims is to create a "memory scene," a big transparent wall blocking the audience's view to start, a living room and dining room, and this picture of a guy in a World War I hat, smiling. He's the absent father. Oh yes, and a typewriter. For kicks.
- Enter Tom Wingfield, dressed as a "merchant sailor" and smoking.
- Turns out the entire play is his memory recreated for us.
- Tom's speech is full of lots of lovely, pedantic metaphors.
- Tom lets us know that his Dad peaced out on them when Tom and his sister Laura were little and sent a postcard that said, "Hello—Goodbye!"
- Did we mention that there's this theatrical device that Williams invented for this play – a big fancy technological thing otherwise known as a "screen"? Words and images get projected onto it. In this first scene, such words happen to be "Ou sont les neiges."
- That phrase is from the title of a poem called "Ou sont les neiges d'antan," which means "where are the snows of yesteryear." So Williams's screen just says "where are the snows." You know, because it's warm in that room.
- Amanda (Tom's mother) annoys Tom at the table with etiquette rules about elbows and not picking his nose.
- Tom retaliates by shouting and then leaving. In other words, aggression for dinner followed by a lovely little passive aggressive tart for dessert.
- Amanda gives the classic "back in the good old days" speech, only she focuses on herself having been a Paris Hilton-esque socialite instead of bread costing twenty cents a loaf.
- In case you missed it, the image of Amanda as a young socialite is projected on the screen.
- Then, because Williams realized he left a word off the first time, the screen now says "Ou sont les neiges d'antan." And if you were wondering, the French still means "where are the snows of yesteryear."
- Amanda expresses not-so-subtly that Laura ought to have some "gentlemen callers." And that she should type on the typewriter.
- We almost forgot. There's this little, light, circus-y tune called "The Glass Menagerie" that gets played every once in a while, usually when the audience is looking at Laura.

Scene Two

- The screen has an image of blue roses.
- Laura is polishing her tiny collection of glass animals (a *glass menagerie* – get it?)
- When Amanda approaches, Laura puts away the glass and pretends she was typing on her typewriter.
- Amanda is thoroughly pissed off. This tends to happen a lot.
- Turns out Laura has been playing hooky from typing school and Amanda just found out at her DAR meeting (Daughters of the American Revolution).
- The screen projects a bunch of typewriters, in case you didn't know what a typewriter looks like.
- Laura gives her excuse: she's painfully shy to the point of nausea and has a crippled leg that makes her hobble.
- Laura responds to the accusations by...playing the Victrola (a CD player but way cooler).
- The screen says "The Crust of Humility."
- Amanda expounds on this crust – it is the result of not marrying, she says.
- Laura reveals that she used to have a crush on this demigod of high school boys, Jim.
- The screen projects a picture of Jim for us.
- Jim used to call her "Blue Roses."
- Amanda denies that Laura is crippled and daydreams about her missing husband's charm.

Scene Three

- There's been a fiasco! Which we know, because the screen says "After the Fiasco."
- Tom chills out on the fire escape and narrates:
- He explains how Amanda wants gentlemen callers for Laura, and an image of...yep, you got it, a gentleman caller appears on the screen.
- Turns out Mrs. Wingfield (that would be Amanda) sells magazine subscriptions.
- Then we see Amanda making these ridiculous phone calls trying to get people to subscribe.
- Screen says, "You think I'm in love with Continental Shoemakers?"
- OK, this is really important: for the next whole conversation, the stage light is on Laura, not the people talking. Got it?
- Amanda and Tom argue because he's been reading the trashy romance novels of D.H. Lawrence. Oh, he also escapes to the movies.
- Tom makes it clear that he hates his job and life in general and wishes someone would come along and bash his brains out. No, literally, he wants someone to bash his brains out, and preferably with a crowbar. Check it out, because we are not making this stuff up.
- He wants to skip town like his father did. Oh, the apple doesn't fall far from the abandonment tree.
- When accused that he's not actually going to the movies, Tom tirades on all the

Satan-worshipping, alcohol-consuming, prostitute-soliciting things he is really doing. That's sarcastic, by the way.
- In a rage, he accidentally breaks several of the glass animals.
- Laura is sad. In a far more eloquent way than this.
- "The Glass Menagerie" music plays again.

Scene Four

- Tom comes home late and drunk and tries to sneak in quietly.
- He runs into Laura and tells her all about the movies and shows he saw and totally ruins the endings for her.
- There is discussion of a coffin and how one might escape from a coffin. Oh, and then the picture of their father lights up.
- The next morning, Tom and Amanda aren't speaking. Ah, family.
- Laura heads out onto the fire escape but slips on her way out.
- The lights illuminate Amanda and "Ave Maria" plays.
- So Tom apologizes, because you can't be angry at a person who makes "Ave Maria" magically come out of the air.
- Amanda discusses the plight of Laura (so she comes up on the screen) and how Tom needs to find her some "gentleman callers." And by that we mean set her up on a date with a boy who doesn't drink.
- She is concerned that Tom is taking after his father.
- Tom defends his nightly movie-going experience. He likes the adventure.
- Amanda calls Tom selfish. Well, actually, she calls him selfish, selfish, selfish in that great, nagging, mothering tone.
- The screen displays the cover of a glamour magazine as Amanda makes more humiliating and pleading phone calls in an attempt to get subscribers.

Scene Five

- Legend on the screen says "Annunciation." This is a biblical reference to when the angel tells Mary she got pregnant and the savior is coming.
- Tom narrates to us about The Paradise Dance Hall across the street from the Wingfield's apartment. He says people go there to escape their mundane lives.
- Amanda joins him in the porch while they discuss Laura – Tom has coerced one of his friends into being a gentleman caller.
- When Tom says this, a blast of music hits the audience. Williams is really into this whole drama thing.
- Amanda is all excited and freaks out because she has to primp herself and her house and her daughter for the big occasion.
- Then she harps on the fact that this guy (with the Irish last name of "O'Connor") better not be a drinker, because Tom's *father* drank and we all know how that turned out.

- The music gets ominous while they discuss Laura and her peculiarities (you know, the glass fetish and the crippled leg).
- Tom goes...to the movies. Where else would he go?
- Amanda and Laura wish on the moon, accompanied by the screen projection of...a moon.

Scene Six

- Tom is smoking on the fire escape again. Man, it's almost like cigarettes are habitually addictive or something.
- Anyway, the screen projects "the high school hero" while Tom narrates about Jim and his many high school hero-related achievements. Basically, Jim was the captain of everything.
- Tom reveals that he and Jim work together at the warehouse, and that Jim has no idea he is being set up with Laura.
- The screen says "The accent of a coming foot."
- Amanda cleaned their house and decked it out for the coming guest.
- Laura's all dolled up, too, or, as Williams so subtly puts it, she is "like a piece of translucent glass."
- Her mom stuffs powder puffs in Laura's top, but only because they didn't have Wonder Bras back then.
- Then Amanda says that pretty women are a trap, and the screen concurs with its caption.
- Laura checks herself out in the mirror while the screen says, "This is my sister: celebrate her with strings." Oh, and there's music, too.
- Amanda gets herself all dressed up, too, harkening back to the days when she was a Southern Belle.
- Laura hears the name of the man coming to call and FLIPS OUT. In case her flip out wasn't dramatic enough, the screen says "Not Jim!"
- It's the same Jim that Laura had a crush on. You got that, yeah?
- Laura sits and is terrified of opening the door when Jim and Tom get there. So the screen says, "The Opening of a Door!" Gasp! Shock!
- The boys show up and Laura is too afraid to answer the door until Amanda verbally abuses her into doing it.
- Cue "Dardanella," a jazzy little number, while she answers the door, shyly greets Jim, and retreats to play the Victrola.
- Jim discusses work with Tom, and how he's taking classes in public speaking and becoming adept at winning friends and influencing people.
- The screen projects an executive sitting at his desk that's supposed to be Jim or something.
- Tom describes the movies and adventure and the good old pirate ship pops up on the screen again while he hints that he may be leaving soon.
- Tom declares he has joined the Union of Merchant Seamen and paid fees to them instead of the light bill.
- Amanda bustles towards the two boys and they're both thinking, "Oh my god, who is this crazy chick?"
- She acts all southern-y while an image of her as a young girl comes up on the screen.

- Laura is all faint and shy and, well, Laura-esque at dinner (the screen reads "terror!" and there's a storm a-rumbling outside), so her mother tells her to lie down in the living room.
- Those not having fainting spells say "Grace" together.

Scene Seven

- The lights go out.
- Amanda asks Tom about paying the light bill and the screen says, "Ha!"
- Amanda sends Jim into the other room to, er...keep Laura company on the couch. Wink wink.
- The screen reads, "I don't suppose you remember me at all!"
- Laura is all hot and bothered. Or maybe just bothered. Laura's on the couch to start off, but Jim has them both sit on the floor.
- Jim's all talkative and breaking through Laura's shy exterior. They reminisce about that time when they barely knew each other and he called her "Blue Roses."
- Laura talks about having a limp from her crippled leg in high school, but Jim says it wasn't noticeable and that she ought to be more outgoing and confident and all that.
- They look together at their old high school yearbook, called "The Torch." Laura praises him for his performance in a high school play and confesses that she used to want his autograph. So Jim graffiti's away on her program (that she saved from his play) with his signature.
- Laura discloses that she dropped out of high school.
- She asks about Jim's old girlfriend, but he says they're not together anymore. You know how high school relationships go.
- Laura is all, "*Hey baby*, want to see my...glass collection?" And the tinkly, thematic music plays again.
- She shows Jim a unicorn, her favorite piece of glass, because its horn makes it different from all the other horses.
- They listen to the music from the Paradise Dance Hall across the street and Jim has them waltz to it.
- During their rambunctious dancing, they break the horn off of the unicorn, but Laura calls it a blessing in disguise.
- Jim hits on Laura. "Blue Roses" comes up on the screen again. He kisses her, exclamation point!
- He backs away and the screen reads "a souvenir."
- Jim gets all awkward and then explains that he has a fiancé named Betty.
- He waxes poetic about love. The screen, very helpfully, says "Love."
- Laura gives him the former-unicorn in its post-horn state as a souvenir.
- Williams gives the director two options for the screen, either "Things have a way of turning out so badly!" or the image of a gentleman caller waving goodbye. Definitely the biggest decision of our day.
- Amanda comes to see how things are moving along and finds out about the engagement just as Jim takes off. The screen says, "The sky falls."
- She yells at Tom after Jim leaves so he takes off for the movies while the screen reads

"and so, goodbye..."
- OK, here's the deal: Tom gives an ending speech while the audience watches Amanda comforting Laura.
- The speech goes something like, "I took off and left my family behind, etc., etc., I couldn't stop feeling guilty about leaving Laura, I can't blow her candles out."
- Then Laura blows the candles out while Jim theatrically says, "And so, goodbye..."

Themes

Theme of Freedom and Confinement

In *The Glass Menagerie*, Tom feels confinement from being stuck in an uninspiring job, cramped into a small apartment with his family, and unable to see the world or have adventures. Amanda is similarly confined to her thoughts of the past, and Laura traps herself in a world of glass animals. Escape can mean two things here: escape from reality into an alternate world, or escape from a trap or confinement. This play hints at the moral ramifications of some kinds of escape, asking the question of who is left behind and what happens to them when you leave.

Questions About Freedom and Confinement

1. Tom talks about getting out of a coffin without removing a nail, which we're pretty sure says something about disrupting his environment by leaving. What is the effect of his leaving, exactly? Did good ol' Tennessee totally rip us off by not letting us see what happened?
2. What is Tom trying to escape from? What exactly is it about his life that bothers him so much?
3. Does Tom *really* escape at the end?
4. Do you totally love the fire escape thing? Because we do. What does it do for the play? We get the escape part - but where's the fire?

Chew on Freedom and Confinement

Tom is a selfish character because of his desire to escape his responsibilities to his family.

Although Tom seeks to escape his life and job at the warehouse, he neither desires nor is able to escape his family.

Theme of Duty

In *The Glass Menagerie*, duty and responsibility largely arise from family. The play examines the conflict between one's obligations and one's real desires, suggesting that being true to one may necessitate abandonment of the other. We also see that duties are gender specific, and arise largely from the expectations of societal norms.

Questions About Duty

1. Amanda says Tom's being selfish. Tom says he's a slave for his family. Chances are, one of them is wrong. But which one? Or are we the ones who are wrong, because somehow both are true?
2. Amanda keeps insisting that a lot of different people have to do a lot of different things. She's taskmaster extraordinaire. So, what exactly does she expect of Tom, of herself, of Laura, of her husband? And where did she get these expectations from?
3. If Tom can't get over leaving Laura, even after many years, is he still in a way responsible to his family, still bound by duties in his mind? How so?

Chew on Duty

Amanda's expectations of Tom are unfair, because she puts all the familial responsibility on his shoulders.

Although Amanda demands a lot of Tom; her expectations of Laura are more unreasonable.

Theme of Family

In *The Glass Menagerie*, family means obligations. This play raises questions of duty and responsibility to your other family members, and for the most part in gender specific roles. We see that it is the job of the male to bring home money, and the daughter to look pretty and get married. This also features the notion of abandonment, as a father leaves the family behind. There is also the notion of children taking after their parents; Tom leaves the family just as his father did, and Amanda wishes her daughter were as popular as she used to be. We see fighting between mother and son over both trivial matters, such as dinner etiquette, and larger issues, such as work and life goals. Lastly, this play examines the relationship between sister and brother, as Tom feels both protective and later guilty with regards to his sister Laura.

Questions About Family

1. This play seems to be saying that you can't choose your family. No kidding. Tom and Amanda are stuck with each other. Do they hate each other? Aren't they supposed to love each other if they're family? Isn't Amanda really just looking out for Tom, in that nagging mother sort of way? Or not?
2. Tom and his father both peace out from the Wingfield family. But in what ways are these situations different? Is Tom really just like his father?
3. What exactly is Tom and Laura's relationship? Because we keep noticing this pattern where Tom breaks her stuff and then stands around and looks at her awkwardly without really saying anything. And what's up with the ending, when he says he was more "faithful" than he intended to be.
4. You might have noticed that Amanda keeps treating her children like they're five-year-olds. Why is that?

Chew on Family

Despite the exaggerated nature of their situation and the hyperbole of their dialogue, actions, and interactions, the Wingfield family in many ways represents the stereotypical American family.

Although Amanda projects her own dreams onto her daughter and son, she is overall a positive force in the lives of her children.

Although Amanda has good intentions, she ends up being a destructive force in the lives of her children.

Theme of Memory and the Past

In *The Glass Menagerie*, memory plays an important part, both thematically and in terms of the play's presentation. Thematically, we see the detrimental effects of memory in the form of Amanda's living in the past. As far as the play's presentation is concerned, the entire story is told from the memory of Tom, the narrator. He makes it clear that, because the play is memory, certain implications are raised as to the nature of each scene. He explains that memory is selective, that events are remembered with music, with peculiar lighting, that reality is altered and edited and made presentable in certain ways. This is how we see the play, directly as a memory.

Questions About Memory and the Past

1. What's the difference between remembering or reminiscing, and then totally living in the past? Where do you draw a line? Or rather, where does Williams choose to draw it?
2. In his production notes, Williams keeps calling this "a memory play," and then talking about lighting and music and all this other funky stuff. Basically the audience never gets to forget they're watching a play, because all these artificial things happen. What do these artificial elements add to the play?

Chew on Memory and the Past

Because the audience is constantly reminded that the play is merely Tom's memory, scenes in *The Glass Menagerie* must necessarily be examined in the light of subjectivity, a lens that changes the way each scene is interpreted.

Theme of Weakness

In *The Glass Menagerie*, weakness is linked to fragility, which comes to mean both beauty and breakability. While Laura's shyness and fragility keep her in her own little world of equally fragile glass animals, they also infuse her with a mysterious individuality, something Jim picks up on with the nickname "Blue Roses" and finds incredibly attractive. Fragility also means dependence, as Laura needs Tom precisely because of her shy and delicate demeanor. We

also see the relationship between physical and mental fragility, as it seems that Laura's shyness arises from a physical defect: her crippled leg.

Questions About Weakness

1. How does Laura's fragility relate to her need to escape reality? Where did it come from? We get some hints of this when she talks about high school…
2. Is Laura the only fragile character in the play? Granted, we pretty much only put quotes about her up there, but hey, what do we know?
3. There's something going on with that unicorn business. Why would it be a blessing in disguise that its horn broke off? Does that mean that Laura secretly wants to be like everyone else?

Chew on Weakness

Despite her attempts at helping, Amanda is the character primarily responsible for Laura's fragility and shyness.

The Glass Menagerie makes it clear that there is no hope for Laura; while Tom escapes, Laura is left stuck in an inescapable rut, a prisoner in her own glass house.

Theme of Deception and Lies

In *The Glass Menagerie*, Amanda retreats from reality by denial and deliberately deluding herself as to the true nature of things. She refuses to see that her daughter is crippled or her son a writer who likes to drink, raising the notion that parents often see only the good qualities in their children. She is also somewhat blind as to her own status; although she readily admits that she is old, Amanda still thinks of herself as the pretty Southern Belle, getting all dolled up and playing the charming hostess.

Questions About Deception and Lies

1. Denial, blindness, self-delusion… EVERYONE in the Wingfield family has jumped onto the escape from reality bandwagon, which is getting pretty crowded. So how does each of them deny the world around them? Which one is worst? Is there ever a good way or reason to enter the world of illusion?
2. We're totally into the scene where Jim penetrates Laura's secret world. Jim is the only character to get through to Laura. What is it about him that lets him do so?

Chew on Deception and Lies

Although Tom, Laura, and Amanda all escape reality and delude themselves, [insert name here] suffers from denial in the most detrimental way.

Although denial may seem detrimental, [insert name here] uses it in a positive and beneficial way.

Theme of Dreams, Hopes, and Plans

In *The Glass Menagerie*, dreams of the future are the source of conflict, primarily when one character's dream doesn't match up with another's. While Amanda wants her children to fulfill the classic American Dream of hard work and success, Tom has dreams of being a writer, and Laura is too shy to even leave the house. This also raises the issue of parents imposing their dreams on their children, rather than allowing them to figure out themselves just what it is that they want.

Questions About Dreams, Hopes, and Plans

1. All these characters, all these dreams. What does each character want?
2. Jim basically has the American Dream, and is doing something about it. How are his efforts presented, though? Does it look like Jim indeed will be successful? Or is there some fun being had at this chipper boy's expense?

Chew on Dreams, Hopes, and Plans

Although their fights take many different forms, Amanda and Tom major conflict is their inability to reconcile their different dreams for the future.

The Glass Menagerie serves as a direct attack on the American Dream, as Amanda's expectations for the marriage and success of her children are impossible.

Theme of Abandonment

In *The Glass Menagerie*, abandonment refers to a member of the family abandoning the family unit, and leaving others behind to fend for themselves. The play deals a little with the moral implications of such an act, as well as the aftermath. It suggests that such an act may be learned from parents, as the son chooses to abandon the family the same way the father did.

Questions About Abandonment

1. What's the difference, for Tom, between abandoning his family and abandoning his life situation (the crumby job, the small town)?
2. Do you hate Tom for abandoning his family? No, really: is he a total jerk? Or is he validated because, honestly, it's *his* life.
3. Why does Tom hold out for so long, and what is the straw that breaks the camels back, that makes him finally leave?

Chew on Abandonment

Because of the nature of son to follow father, Tom cannot be held responsible for following in his father's footsteps and abandoning his family.

The Glass Menagerie fails to provide adequate reasoning to explain Tom's sudden departure from the family.

Theme of Marriage

In *The Glass Menagerie*, marriage is used as a tool rather than a celebration of love. Amanda believes that marriage is a necessary step for her daughter to live comfortably, to be supported by a man. This play also calls into question the lasting nature of marriage, as the marriage of the mother figure (Amanda) and her missing husband has been destroyed by his abandonment of her.

Questions About Marriage

1. What does marriage mean to Amanda? Why does she want Laura to get married?
2. What exactly is going on with Amanda's husband? She only says nice things about him (except for the whole drinking part). So how does she feel about being abandoned by him? Is she hiding something?

Chew on Marriage

Because Amanda is unable to necessarily tie love to the institution of marriage, she sees it as a tool of manipulation rather than a mutual decision.

Theme of Gender

In *The Glass Menagerie*, gender roles play a large part in dictating the future plans of each character. Laura must get married because she is a girl; Tom should take business classes because he is a man. Gender roles seem to arise from tradition, as Amanda discusses what women should do and what men should do according to her Southern upbringing. Gender roles also dictate values, or how women and men are judged differently. Amanda places great importance on Laura's staying 'fresh and pretty,' while she believes that 'character' is the most important thing for a man.

Questions About Gender

1. What's Amanda's deal with gender roles? What with the husband having to support EVERYONE and the girl having to look pretty ALL THE TIME? Where is she getting this from, and what kind of effect does it have on her children?
2. Do Tom and Laura reject or assimilate the gender roles projected on them?

Chew on Gender

Although they resist the roles prescribed to them, Laura and Tom both eventually assimilate to the gender stereotypes cast by their mother.

Theme of Love

In *The Glass Menagerie*, love is tricky. We're never really sure if love is genuine, or convenient, if it's really love, or whether it's just infatuation. The closest thing there is to genuine love occurs between Laura and Jim, and is based on a mutual understanding of each other's individuality and uniqueness. Jim's supposed love for Betty and their impending marriage is based on them 'getting along fine,' and while Amanda confesses that she loved her missing husband, he abandoned her, calling into question just how mutual that love was from the start. There is also the issue of familial love, and how to reconcile the anger and frustration we may feel with family members with our innate love for them. Particularly explored here is the nature of love between brother and sister, who support each other when on rocky ground with their mother.

Questions About Love

1. Amanda said she loved Tom's father, and she says it like it's a state secret, even though they were married. So…did she love him? How does that affect how she feels about his having abandoned her?
2. You've got your romantic love on one hand and then you've got your family love on the other hand. How do these two different types of love manifest themselves in this play. Is one stronger? Are they ever in competition?

Chew on Love

While Amanda discusses her marriage to her missing husband, Laura her infatuation for Jim, and Jim his feelings for his fiancée, none of these characters actually experiences genuine love.

Theme of Drugs and Alcohol

In *The Glass Menagerie*, alcoholism is not major or explicit, yet becomes a symbol for all undesirable activities. Amanda uses alcohol as an umbrella to cover any un-ambitious activities that her son takes part in, including writing, reading, and going to the movies. When she asks if Laura's gentleman caller is a "boy who drinks," what she really wants to know is whether he is the kind of boy who drinks, is rowdy, goes out at night, and doesn't care too much about his future. Because her husband drank, Amanda associates alcoholism with him, and therefore with irresponsibility and abandonment.

Questions About Drugs and Alcohol

1. So, we called it alcoholism, but is it really? Is Tom really an alcoholic? Was his father? And why is Amanda so obsessed with it?
2. We do see some evidence that Tom drinks, namely the drunken stupor and the empty bottle. What does this have to do with his trying to escape?

Chew on Drugs and Alcohol

Because it is the one fault she claims of her missing husband, Amanda sees alcoholism as the root of all evil, using it as an overarching umbrella to characterize everything that she believes is wrong about Tom's way of living.

Quotes

Freedom and Confinement Quotes

The Wingfield apartment is in the rear of the building, one of those vast hive-like conglomerations of cellular living-units that flower as warty growths in overcrowded urban centers of lower middle-class populations and are symptomatic of the impulse of this largest and fundamentally enslaved section of American society to avoid fluidity and differentiation and to exist and function as one interfused mass of automatism. (stage directions, 1.1)

Thought: Williams uses a description of the setting to establish the prison-like feel the Wingfield apartment takes on for Tom.

The apartment faces an alley and is entered by a fire escape, a structure whose name is a touch of accidental poetic truth, for all of these large buildings are always burning with the slow and implacable fires of human desperation. The fire escape is part of what we see - that is, the landing of it and steps descending from it. (stage directions, 1.2)

Thought: The fire escape attached to the apartment speaks to Tom's desired escape from the family.

"A blown-up photograph of the father hangs on the wall of the living room, to the left of the archway. It is the face of a very handsome young man in a doughboy's First World War cap. He is gallantly smiling, ineluctably smiling, as if to say "I will be smiling forever." (stage directions, Scene One).

Thought: While Tom is at first presented as confined to the Wingfield apartment, his father has already made the escape that Tom will later make (unsuccessfully) himself.

Tom enters, dressed as a merchant sailor, and strolls across to the fire escape. There he stops and lights a cigarette. He addresses the audience. (stage directions, Scene One).

Thought: Tom's attire at the outset of the play highlights his having escaped – from the apartment and the family.

There is a fifth character in the play who doesn't appear except in this larger-than-life-size photograph over the mantel. This is our father who left us a long time ago. He was a telephone man who fell in love with long distances; he gave up his job with the telephone company and skipped the light fantastic out of town...

The last we heard of him was a picture postcard from Mazatlan, on the Pacific coast of Mexico, containing a message of two words: "Hello - Goodbye!" and no address. (1.1, Tom).

Thought: Tom's father displays no guilt at having made his escape from the family.

Tom speaks from the fire escape landing. (Scene Three, stage directions.)

Thought: Tom the narrator often speaks from the fire escape, emphasizing that, at the time he tells the story, he is no longer confined to the apartment and family.

"Look! I've got no thing, no single thing...

...in my life that I can call my OWN! Everything is...

...Yesterday you confiscated my books!" (3.11, 3.13, 3.15, Tom).

Thought: Tom feels confined not only because of his job and position as breadwinner, but because of Amanda's added restrictions on his life.

"House, house! Who pays rent on it, who makes a slave of himself to—" (3.17, Tom).

Thought: Tom uses hyperbole to emphasize the overwhelming sense of imprisonment he feels.

"What do you think I'm at? Aren't I supposed to have any patience to reach the end of, Mother? I know, I know. It seems unimportant to you, what I'm doing – what I want to do – having a little difference between them!" (3.30, Tom).

Thought: Tom is trapped not only by his confining situation, but also by his mother's inability to recognize his desires.

"Listen! You think I'm crazy about the warehouse? [He bends fiercely toward her slight figure.] You think I'm in love with Continental Shoemakers? You think that I want to spend fifty-five years down there in that – celotex interior! with—fluorescent—tubes! Look! I'd rather somebody packed up a crowbar and battered out my brains—than go back mornings! I go! Every time you come in yelling that Goddamn 'Rise and Shine! Rise and Shine!' I say to myself, 'How lucky dead people are!' But I get up. I go! For sixty-five dollars a month I give up all that I dream of doing and being ever! And you say self—self's all I ever think of! Why, listen, if self is what I thought of, Mother, I'd be where he is—GONE! [He points to his father's picture.] As far as the system of transportation reaches!" (3.34, Tom).

Thought: Tom uses hyperbole to emphasize the overwhelming sense of imprisonment he feels.

"Where have you been all this time?"

"I have been to the movies."

"All this time at the movies?"

"There was a very long program. There was a Garbo picture and a Mickey Mouse and a travelogue and a newsreel and a preview of coming attractions. And there was an organ solo and a collection for the Milk Fund—simultaneously—which ended up in a terrible fight between a fat lady and an usher!" (4.7).

Thought: Just as Laura uses the glass menagerie as a means of escape from reality, so Tom uses the movies.

"And, oh, I forgot! There was a big stage show! The headliner on this stage show was Malvolio the Magician…But the wonderfullest trick of all was the coffin trick. We nailed him into a coffin and hr got out of the coffin without removing one nail. There is trick that would come in handy for me—get me out of this two-by-four situation!

[…] "You know it don't take much intelligence to get yourself into a nailed-up coffin, Laura. But who the hell ever got himself out of one without removing one nail?" (4.9, 4.13, Tom).

Thought: Tom recognizes that to escape from his own coffin of his job, apartment, and family obligations, he would have to upset his surroundings.

"And you-when I see you taking after his ways! Staying out late-and-well, you had been drinking the night you were in that-terrifying condition! Laura says that you hate the apartment and that you go out nights to get away from it! Is that true, Tom?" (4.63, Amanda).

Thought: Laura recognizes Tom's desires more clearly than does Amanda.

"But why—why, Tom—are you always so restless? Where do you go to, nights?

"I—go to the movies."

"Why do you go to the movies so much, Tom?"

"I go to the movies because—I like adventure. Adventure is something I don't have much of at work, so I go to the movies." (4.65-4.68).

Thought: Tom seeks from the movies what his own life lacks, and thus uses them as a means to escape from the confines of his daily goings-on.

"Man is by instinct a lover, a hunter, a fighter, and none of those instincts are given much play at the warehouse!" (4.76, Tom).

Thought: Tom seeks escape to the life he believes he was meant to lead.

"Across the alley from us was the Paradise Dance Hall. On evenings in the spring the windows and doors were open and the music came outdoors. Sometimes the lights were turned out except for a large glass sphere that hung from the ceiling. It would turn rather slowly about and filter the dusk with delicate rainbow colors. Then the orchestra would play a waltz or a tango, something that had a slow and sensuous rhythm. Couples would come outside, to the relative privacy of the alley. You would see them kissing behind ash pits and telephone poles. This was the compensation for lives that passed like mine, without any change or adventure. Adventure and change were imminent this year. They were waiting around the corner for all these kids. Suspended in the mist over Berchtesgaden, caught in the folds of Chamberlain's umbrella. In Spain there was Guernica. But here there was only hot swing music and liquor, dance halls, bars, and movies, and sex that hung in the gloom like a chandelier and flooded the world with brief, deceptive rainbows…All the world was waiting for bombardments! (5.10, Tom).

Thought: Tom recognizes that many others, not just he himself, use dancing and movies as a means to escape the reality of their own lives.

"You and me, we're not the warehouse type." (6.84, Jim).

Thought: Jim and Tom find camaraderie in their both wanting to escape.

"I'm planning to change." [He leans over the fire-escape rail, speaking with quiet exhilaration. The incandescent marquees and signs of the first-run movie houses light his face from across the alley. He looks like a voyager.] "I'm right at the point of committing myself to a future that doesn't include the warehouse and Mr. Mendoza or even a night-school course in public speaking." (6.110, Tom, Scene Six stage directions).

Thought: Tom plots his escape well in advance; therefore his abandoning the family is a pre-meditated act, not something executed in the heat of an argument.

"Yes, movies! Look at them—[a wave toward the marvels of Grand Avenue]. All of those glamorous people—having adventures—hogging it all, gobbling the whole thing up! You know what happens? People go to the movies instead of moving! Hollywood characters are supposed to have all the adventures for everybody in America, while everybody in America sits in a dark room and watches them have them! Yes, until there's a war. That's when adventure becomes available to the masses! Everyone's dish, not only Gable's! Then the people in the dark room come out of the dark room to have some adventures themselves—goody, goody! It's our turn now, to go to the South Sea Island—to make a safari—to be exotic, far off! But I'm not patient. I don't want to wait till then. I'm tired of the movies and I am about to move! (6.114, Tom).

Thought: Tom is so dissatisfied at his confinement that he would even prefer war to staying at home.

"I'm starting to boil inside. I know I seem dreamy, but inside—well, I'm boiling! Whenever I pick up a shoe, I shudder a little thinking how short life is and what am I doing! Whatever that means, I know it doesn't mean shoes—except as something to wear on a traveler's feet!" (6.120, Tom).

Thought: Tom describes his desire to escape in a way that makes him sound a victim helpless to his impulses, rather than a conscious, decision-making adult.

Tom smashes his glass on the floor. He plunges out on the fire escape, slamming the door. Laura screams in fright. The dance-hall music becomes louder. Tom stands on the fire escape, gripping the rail. The moon breaks through the storm clouds, illuminating his face. (Scene Seven, stage directions.)

Thought: Tom spends a lot of time on the fire escape, foreshadowing his eventual departure.

"I didn't go to the moon – I went much further—for time is the longest distance between two poles. Not long after that I was fired for writing a poem on the lid of a shoe-box. I left St. Louis. I descended the steps of this fire escape for a last time and followed, from then on, in my father's footsteps, attempting to find in motion what was lost in space." (7.321, Tom).

Thought: Although they differ in their emotional responses to escape, Tom makes it clear that he left the Wingfield apartment in much the same way his father did.

"Then all at once my sister touches my shoulder. I turn around and look into her eyes. Oh, Laura, Laura, I tried to leave you behind me, but I am more faithful than I intended to be! I reach for a cigarette, I cross the street, I run into the movies or a bar, I buy a drink, I speak to the nearest anything-anything that can blow your candles out! For nowadays the world is lit by lightning! Blow out your candles, Laura-and so, goodbye… (7.321, Tom).

Thought: Although he is able to literally escape the Wingfield apartment, Tom is never able to completely escape the ties of his familial obligations to Laura.

Duty Quotes

A blown-up photograph of the father hangs on the wall of the living room, to the left of the archway. It is the face of a very handsome young man in a doughboy's First World War cap. He is gallantly smiling, ineluctably smiling, as if to say "I will be smiling forever." (stage directions, Scene One).

Thought: Unlike Tom, Tom's father seems to have shirked his responsibilities without thought or regret.

"There is a fifth character in the play who doesn't appear except in this larger-than-life-size photograph over the mantel. This is our father who left us a long time ago. He was a telephone man who fell in love with long distances; he gave up his job with the telephone company and skipped the light fantastic out of town…

The last we heard of him was a picture postcard from Mazatlan, on the Pacific coast of Mexico, containing a message of two words: "Hello - Goodbye!" and no address." (1.1, Tom).

Thought: Again, Tom's father doesn't seem to regret abandoning his family.

"They knew how to entertain their gentlemen callers. It wasn't enough for a girl to be possessed of a pretty face and a graceful figure - although I wasn't slighted in either respect. She also needed to have a nimble wit and a tongue to meet all occasions." (1.27, Amanda).

Thought: Amanda believes that, while men have the responsibility of bringing home money, women, too, have duties to fulfill.

"I know so well what becomes of unmarried woman who aren't prepared to occupy a position. I've seen such pitiful cases in the South - barely tolerated spinsters living upon the grudging patronage of sister's husband or brother's wife! - stuck away in some little mousetrap of a

room - encouraged by one in-law to visit another - little birdlike women without any nest - eating the crust of humility all their life!

Is that the future that we've mapped out for ourselves? I swear it's the only alternative I can think of! [She pauses.] It isn't a very pleasant alternative, is it? [She pauses again.] Of course - some girls do marry." (2.34, Amanda).

Thought: Amanda believes it is a woman's duty to marry.

"House, house! Who pays rent on it, who makes a slave of himself to—" (3.17, Tom).

Thought: Tom makes it clear that he is fulfilling his responsibilities at the moment.

"What right have you got to jeopardize your job? Jeopardize the security of us all? How do you think we'd manage if you were—" (3.33, Amanda)

Thought: Amanda believes that, since her husband left, Tom is responsible for their family.

She crosses through the portieres and draws them together behind her. Tom is left with Laura. Laura clings weakly to the mantel with her face averted. Tom stares at her stupidly for a moment. Then he crosses to the shelf. He drops awkwardly on his knees to collect the fallen glass, glancing at Laura as if he would speak but couldn't. (Scene Three, stage directions).

Thought: Even when he is fighting with their mother, Tom never wavers in his care for Laura. This is one duty he never fails to fulfill.

Tom glances sheepishly but sullenly at her averted figure and slumps at the table…Tom blows on his coffee, glancing sidewise at his mother. She clears her throat. Tom clears his throat…

[hoarsely]: "Mother. I—I apologize, Mother." (Scene Four stage directions, 4.32, Tom).

Thought: Tom's responsibility is not only to support the family financially, but to hold it together emotionally.

"I've had to put up a solitary battle all these years. But you're my right-hand bower! Don't fall down, don't fail!" (4.37, Amanda).

Thought: Amanda places the responsibility on Tom to hold the family together.

"We have to do all that we can to build ourselves up. In these trying times we live in, all that we have to cling to is-each other…" (4.51, Amanda).

Thought: Amanda believes that all members of the family have an obligation to each other

"However, you do act strangely. I—I'm not criticizing, understand that! I know your ambitions do not lie in the warehouse, that like everybody in the whole wide world—you've had to—make sacrifices, but—Tom—Tom—life's not easy, it calls for—Spartan endurance!" (4.61).

Thought: Amanda believes that duty and responsibility are more important than one's own dreams.

"Oh, I can see the handwriting on the wall as plain as I can see the nose in front of my face! It's terrifying! More and more you remind me of your father! He was out all hours without explanation!-Then left! Goodbye! And me with the bag to hold. I saw that letter you got from the Merchant Marine. I know what you're dreaming of. I'm not standing here blindfolded. Very well, then. Then do it! But not till there's somebody to take your place." (4.91, Amanda).

Thought: Amanda believes that duty and responsibility are more important than one's own dreams.

"I mean that as soon as Laura has got somebody to take care of her, married, a home of her own, independent-why, then you'll be free to go wherever you please, on land, on sea, whichever way the wind blows you! But until that time you've got to look out for your sister. I don't say me because I'm old and don't matter! I say for your sister because she's young and dependent." (4.93, Amanda).

Thought: Amanda focuses on Tom's obligation to his sister, rather than to herself.

"What can I do about it?"

"Overcome selfishness! Self, self, self, is that all you ever think of?" (4.94, 4.95, Tom and Amanda).

Thought: Amanda constantly berates Tom for his dreams and ambitions.

"We are going to have one."

"What?"

"A gentleman caller!" (5. 30-5.32).

Thought: Tom fulfills the family duty of bringing home a man for Laura.

"You don't have to make any fuss."

"Oh, Tom, Tom, Tom, of course I have to make a fuss! I want things nice. not sloppy! Not thrown together. I'll certainly have to do some fast thinking, won't I?"

…

"You just don't know. We can't have a gentleman caller in a pigsty! All my wedding silver has to be polished, the monogrammed table linen ought to be laundered! The windows have to be washed and fresh curtains put up. And how about clothes? We have to wear something, don't we?" (5.57, 5.59, Amanda).

Thought: While Amanda believes it is Tom's duty to bring home money, she takes on for herself many home-related tasks.

"I paid my dues this month, instead of the light bill."

"You will regret it when they turn the lights off."

"I won't be here." (6. 124-6.126, Tom and Jim).

Thought: In contrast to Amanda's selflessness, Tom at moments does indeed appear to be selfish.

"That's right, now that you've had us all make such fools of ourselves. The effort, the preparations, all the expense! The new floor lamp, the rug, the clothes for Laura! All for what? To entertain some other girl's fiancé! Go to the movies, go! Don't think about us, an unmarried sister who's crippled and has no job! Don't let anything interfere with your selfish pleasure! Just go, go, go—to the movies!" (7.319, Amanda).

Thought: Because Jim was engaged, Amanda believes that Tom has failed to fulfill his obligations to the family.

"GO, then! Go to the moon—you selfish dreamer!" (7.320, Amanda).

Thought: Amanda views even the small pleasure of going out at night as a selfish endeavor.

"Then all at once my sister touches my shoulder. I turn around and look into her eyes. Oh, Laura, Laura, I tried to leave you behind me, but I am more faithful than I intended to be! I reach for a cigarette, I cross the street, I run into the movies or a bar, I buy a drink, I speak to the nearest anything-anything that can blow your candles out! For nowadays the world is lit by lightning! Blow out your candles, Laura-and so, goodbye… (7.321, Tom).

Thought: Although he tries to escape his responsibility to his family through geographical distance, Tom never escapes the chains of family obligation.

Family Quotes

"A blown-up photograph of the father hangs on the wall of the living room, to the left of the archway. It is the face of a very handsome young man in a doughboy's First World War cap. He is gallantly smiling, ineluctably smiling, as if to say, "I will be smiling forever." (stage directions, Scene One).

Thought: Although he is absent physically, Tom and Laura's father remains an ever-present member of the family.

There is a fifth character in the play who doesn't appear except in this larger-than-life-size photograph over the mantel. This is our father who left us a long time ago. He was a telephone man who fell in love with long distances; he gave up his job with the telephone company and skipped the light fantastic out of town…

The last we heard of him was a picture postcard from Mazatlan, on the Pacific coast of Mexico, containing a message of two words: "Hello – Goodbye!" and no address. (1.1, Tom).

Thought: Tom's father has failed to fit the traditional role of father in the Wingfield family.

"Honey, don't push with your fingers. If you have to push something, the thing to push with is a crust of bread. And chew - chew! Animals have secretions in their stomach which enable them to digest food without mastication, but human beings are supposed to chew their food before they swallow it down. Eat food leisurely, son, and really enjoy it. A well-cooked meal has lots of delicate flavors that have to be held in the mouth for appreciation. So chew your food and give your salivary glands a chance to function!" (1.6, Amanda).

Thought: Amanda takes on an extremely mothering role towards her children, treating them as though they were still young.

"I haven't enjoyed one bite of this dinner because of your constant directions on how to eat it. It's you that make me rush through meals with your hawklike attention to every bite I take. Sickening - spoils my appetite - all this discussion of - animals' secretion - salivary glands - mastication!" (1.7, Tom).

Thought: Tom rebels against Amanda's mothering as though he were a young child.

"You smoke too much." (1.10, Amanda). Amanda constantly harps on Tom with orders and complaints.

"I know what's coming!"

`*"Yes, but let her tell it."*

"Again?"

"She loves to tell it."

(1.17-1.20, Tom and Laura).

Thought: Laura has a great understanding of her mother and brothers, and often serves as referee between them.

"It isn't a flood, it's not a tornado, Mother. I'm just not popular like you were in Blue Mountain." (1.38, Laura).

Thought: Laura and Amanda, because of their roles as mother and daughter, are often compared.

Seeing her mother's expression, Laura touches her lips with a nervous gesture. (Scene Two, stage directions).

Thought: Laura feels guilty for being unable to please her mother.

"Oh! I felt so weak I could barely keep on my feet! I had to sit down while they got me a glass of water! Fifty dollars' tuition, all of our plans - my hopes and ambitions for you - just gone up the spout, just gone up the spout like that." (2.16, Amanda).

Thought: Amanda fails in her attempts to mold her children as she desires.

"Mother, when you're disappointed, you get that awful suffering look on your face, like the picture of Jesus' mother in the museum!" (2.31, Laura).

Thought: Laura often displays her insight into her mother's moods and actions.

[in a tone of frightened apology]: "I'm crippled!"

"Nonsense, Laura, I've told you never, never to use that word. Why, you're not crippled, you just have a little defect - hardly noticeable, even! When people have some slight disadvantage like that, they cultivate other things to make up for it - develop charm - and vivacity - and - charm! That's all you have to do!" (2.47-2.50, Laura and Amanda).

Thought: Amanda has a mother's unconditional love for her children, so much so that she is unable to see anything wrong with her daughter.

"Don't you use that—"

"—supposed to do!"

"—expression, Not in my—"

"Ohhh!"

"—presence! Have you gone out of your senses?"

"I have, that's true, driven out!" (3.4-3.9, Amanda and Tom).

Thought: Tom and Amanda frequently argue in stereotypical yelling matches of mother and son.

"You will hear more, you—"

"No, I won't hear more, I'm going out!"

"You come right back in—"

"Out, out, out! Because I'm—"

"Come back here, Tom Wingfield! I'm not through talking to you!"

"Oh, go—"

[desperately]: "--Tom!" (3.22-3.28, Amanda, Tom, and Laura).

Thought: Laura watches helplessly as Tom and Amanda fight with each other.

She crosses through the portieres and draws them together behind her. Tom is left with Laura. Laura clings weakly to the mantel with her face averted. Tom stares at her stupidly for a moment. Then he crosses to the shelf. He drops awkwardly on his knees to collect the fallen glass, glancing at Laura as if he would speak but couldn't. (Scene Three, stage directions).

Thought: Even while he is fighting with his mother, Tom maintains family loyalty and love for his sister.

[beseechingly]: "Tom, speak to Mother this morning. Make up with her, apologize, speak to her!" (4.16, Laura)

Thought: Laura frequently tries to intervene in Tom and Amanda's fights.

A second later she cries out. Tom springs up and crosses to the door. Tom opens the door.

"Laura?"

"I'm all right. I slipped, but I'm all right." (Scene Four stage directions, 4.29, 4.30, Tom and Laura).

Thought: Tom displays a brotherly concern and protective attitude toward his sister Laura.

[hoarsely]: "Mother. I—I apologize, Mother."

Amanda draws a quick, shuddering breath. Her face works grotesquely. She breaks into childlike tears.

"I'm sorry for what I said, for everything that I said, I didn't mean it."

[sobbingly]: "My devotion has made me a witch and so I make myself hateful to my children!" (4.32, Tom, Scene Four stage directions, 4.33, Amanda).

Thought: Amanda struggles with doing what she believes is best for her children.

[with great enthusiasm]: "Try and you will succeed! [The notion makes her breathless.] Why, you – you're just full of natural endowments! Both of my children—they're unusual children! Don't you think I know it? I'm so—proud! Happy and—feel I've—so much to be thankful for…" (4.39, Amanda).

Thought: Amanda has a mother's unconditional love for her children, so much so that she is unable to see anything wrong with her children.

"You can't put in a day's work on an empty stomach. You've got ten minutes—don't gulp! Drinking too-hot liquids makes cancer of the stomach…Put cream in." (4.47, Amanda).

Thought: Amanda, in her mothering, treats Tom as though he were a child.

"We have to do all that we can to build ourselves up. In these trying times we live in, all that we have to cling to is—each other…" (4.51, Amanda).

Thought: Amanda sees the family as a unit of support during tough times.

"A few days ago I came in and she was crying."

"What about?"

"You."

"Me?"

"She has an idea that you're not happy here." (4.55-4.59, Amanda and Tom).

Thought: Just as Tom displays a brotherly concern for Laura, so she feels the same love and concern for her brother.

"And you—when I see you taking after his ways! Staying out late—and—well, you had been drinking the night you were in that—terrifying condition! Laura says that you hate the apartment and that you go out nights to get away from it! Is that true, Tom?" (4.63, Amanda).

Thought: While Amanda wants Laura to be more like she was, she fears that Tom will become like his father.

"Oh, I can see the handwriting on the wall as plain as I can see the nose in front of my face! It's terrifying! More and more you remind me of your father! He was out all hours without explanation!-Then left! Goodbye! And me with the bag to hold. I saw that letter you got from the Merchant Marine. I know what you're dreaming of. I'm not standing here blindfolded. Very well, then. Then do it! But not till there's somebody to take your place." (4.91, Amanda).

Thought: While Amanda wants Laura to be more like she was, she fears that Tom will become like his father.

"I mean that as soon as Laura has got somebody to take care of her, married, a home of her own, independent-why, then you'll be free to go wherever you please, on land, on sea, whichever way the wind blows you! But until that time you've got to look out for your sister. I don't say me because I'm old and don't matter! I say for your sister because she's young and dependent." (4.93, Amanda).

Thought: Despite all her nagging and otherwise unappealing qualities, Amanda displays a real selflessness with regard to her place in the Wingfield family.

"Where is your muffler! Put your wool muffler on!" (4.95, Amanda).

Thought: Amanda treats Tom as though he were a child.

"There is only one respect in which I would like you to emulate your father."

"What respect is that?"

"The care he always took of his appearance. He never allowed himself to look untidy." (5.3-5.5, Amanda and Tom).

Thought: Amanda repeatedly compares Tom to his father.

"I'll tell you what I wished for on the moon. Success and happiness for my precious children! I wish for that whenever there's a moon, and when there isn't a moon, I wish for it, too." (5.23, Amanda).

Thought: Amanda's maternal instincts direct her every thought and desire.

"What are you doing?"

"I'm brushing that cowlick down! [She attacks his hair with the brush.] (5.82, 5.83, Tom and Amanda).

Thought: Amanda treats Tom as though he were a child.

"Laura seems all those things to you and me because she's ours and we love her. We don't even notice she's crippled anymore." (5.122, Tom).

Thought: Tom recognizes that familial love can be blinding and misleading.

"Laura Wingfield, you march right to that door!"

"Yes—yes, Mother!" (6.60, 6.61, Amanda and Laura).

Thought: Amanda orders and disciplines her children as though they were very young.

"How about your mother?"

"I'm like my father. The bastard son of a bastard! Did you notice how he's grinning in his picture in there? And he's been absent going in sixteen years!" (6.127, 6.128, Jim and Tom).

Thought: Tom recognizes that he has become similar to his father.

"That's right, now that you've had us all make such fools of ourselves. The effort, the preparations, all the expense! The new floor lamp, the rug, the clothes for Laura! All for what? To entertain some other girl's fiancé! Go to the movies, go! Don't think about us, an unmarried sister who's crippled and has no job! Don't let anything interfere with your selfish pleasure! Just go, go, go-to the movies!" (7.319, Amanda).

Thought: Amanda believes that being a member of a family generates certain obligations.

Tom's closing speech is timed with what is happening inside the house. We see, as though through soundproof glass, that Amanda appears to be making a comforting speech to Laura, who is huddled upon the sofa. Now that we cannot hear the mother's speech, she lifts her head to smile at her mother. Amanda's gestures are slow and graceful, almost dance-like, as she comforts her daughter. At the end of the speech she glances a moment at the father's picture—then withdraws through the portieres. At the close of Tom's speech, Laura blows out the candles, ending the play.

Although Amanda often nags and bother her children, her very maternal instincts take on a positive light in the direst of circumstances

"I didn't go to the moon - I went much further-for time is the longest distance between two poles. Not long after that I was fired for writing a poem on the lid of a shoe-box. I left St. Louis. I descended the steps of this fire escape for a last time and followed, from then on, in my father's footsteps, attempting to find in motion what was lost in space." (7.321, Tom).

Thought: Tom recognizes that he is like his father.

"Then all at once my sister touches my shoulder. I turn around and look into her eyes. Oh, Laura, Laura, I tried to leave you behind me, but I am more faithful than I intended to be! I reach for a cigarette, I cross the street, I run into the movies or a bar, I buy a drink, I speak to the nearest stranger-anything that can blow your candles out! For nowadays the world is lit by lightning! Blow out your candles, Laura--and so, goodbye… (7.321, Tom).

Thought: Tom is unable to relieve the guilt of having abandoned his sister.

Memory and the Past Quotes

The audience hears and sees the opening scene in the dining room through both the transparent fourth wall of the building and the transparent gauze portieres of the dining-room arch. It is during this revealing scene that the fourth wall slowly ascends, out of sight. This transparent exterior wall is not brought down again until the very end of the play, during Tom's final speech. (Stage directions, Scene One).

Thought: Williams uses many visual devices to create a scene of memory, rather than live action or fact.

Yes, I have tricks in my pocket, I have things u p my sleeve. But I am the opposite of a stage magician. He gives you illusion that has the appearance of truth. I give you truth in the pleasant disguise of illusion. (1.1, Tom).

Thought: It is interesting that Tom claims that his altered memory scene is truth in the disguise of illusion, since all of Amanda's reminiscence of the past is illusion in a mask of truth. This begs the question as to how accurately this narrator Tom is revealing his story.

A blown-up photograph of the father hangs on the wall of the living room, to the left of the archway. It is the face of a very handsome young man in a doughboy's First World War cap. He is gallantly smiling, ineluctably smiling, as if to say "I will be smiling forever." (stage directions, Scene One).

Thought: Just as the portrait of Amanda's husband hangs in the house, so does the past (when he was there in person) hover over the present of the play.

To begin with, I turn back time. I reverse it to that quaint period, the thirties, where the huge middle class of America was matriculating in a school for the blind. Their eyes had failed them, or they had failed their eyes, and so they were having their fingers pressed forcibly down on the fiery Braille alphabet of a dissolving economy. (1.1, Tom).

Thought: Because of the narrative nature of the play, issues of the past and future necessarily dominate.

Legend on screen: "Ou sont les neiges." (Scene One, stage directions).

Thought: The legend reading, "Where are the snows of yesteryear," in French underscores Amanda's longing for the past.

To begin with, I turn back time. I reverse it to that quaint period, the thirties, where the huge middle class of America was matriculating in a school for the blind. Their eyes had failed them, or they had failed their eyes, and so they were having their fingers pressed forcibly down on the fiery Braille alphabet of a dissolving economy. (1.1, Tom).

Thought: The elaborate and flowery descriptions in the play can be attributed to the nature of its narrator, Tom, who recalls the scenes, poeticized, from his memory.

The play is memory. Being a memory play, it is dimly lighted, it is sentimental, it is not realistic. In memory everything seems to happen to music. That explains the fiddle in the wings. (1.1, Tom).

Thought: Williams uses light to emphasize the subjective and memory nature of the play.

The scene is memory and therefore nonrealistic. Memory takes a lot of poetic license. It omits some details; others are exaggerated according to the emotional value of the articles it touches, for memory is seated predominantly in the heart. The interior is therefore rather dim and poetic. (stage directions, 1.3)

Thought: The nature of memory is not only a central theme in the play itself, but also dictates the way in which the play is presented to the audience.

"Sometimes they come when they are least expected! Why, I remember one Sunday afternoon in Blue Mountain-" (1.16, Amanda).

Thought: To Amanda, memory has a detrimental effect, dragging her away from reality to live in the past.

"One Sunday afternoon in Blue Mountain - your mother received - seventeen! - gentlemen callers! Why, sometimes there weren't enough chairs to accommodate them all. We had to send the nigger over to bring in folding chairs from the parish house." (1.21, Amanda).

Thought: The believability of Amanda's stories is brought into question.

"Girls in those days knew how to talk, I can tell you." (1.25, Amanda).

Thought: Amanda finds the standards of her present to be inadequate when measured by those of her past.

"There was young Champ Laughlin who later became vice president of the Delta Planters Bank. Hadley Stevenson who was drowned in Moon Lake and left his widow one hundred and fifty thousand in government bonds. There were the Cutrere brothers, Wesley and Bates. Bates was one of my bright particular beaux! He got in a quarrel with that wild Wainwright boy. They shot it out on the floor of Moon Lake Casino. Bates was shot through the stomach. Died in the ambulance on his way to Memphis. His widow was also well provided-for, came into eight or ten thousand acres, that's all. She married him on the rebound - never loved her - carried my picture on him the night he died! And there was that boy that every girl in the Delta had set her cap for! That beautiful, brilliant young Fitzhugh boy from Green County!" (1.29, Amanda).

Thought: For Amanda, all memory is infused with a twinge of regret.

"No, dear, you go in front and study your typewriter chart. Or practice your shorthand a little. Stay fresh and pretty! - It's almost time for our gentlemen callers to start arriving. [She flounces girlishly toward the kitchenette] How many do you suppose we're going to entertain this afternoon?" (1.35, Amanda).

Thought: Amanda's movements and body language strengthen the notion that she is living in her own past.

She has on one of those cheap or imitation velvety-looking cloth coats with imitation fur collar. Her hat is five or six years old, one of those dreadful cloche hats that were worn in the late Twenties, and she is clutching an enormous black patent leather pocketbook with nickel clasps and initials. This is her full-dress outfit, the one she usually wears to the D.A.R. (Scene Two, stage directions).

Thought: Amanda's clothes strengthen the notion that she is living in her own past.

He tears the portieres open. The dining-room area is lit with a turgid smoky red glow. (Scene Three, stage directions).

Thought: Williams uses light to emphasize the subjective and memory nature of the play.

"I was valuable to him as someone who could remember his former glory." (6.1, Tom).

Thought: Jim, like Amanda, revels in the memory of his glory days.

The light dims out on Tom and comes up in the Wingfield living room—a delicate lemony light. It is abut five on a Friday evening of late spring which comes "scattering poems in the sky. (Scene Six stage directions).

Thought: Williams uses light to emphasize the subjective and memory nature of the play.

A faraway, scratchy rendition of 'Dardanella" softens the air and gives her strength to move through it. (Scene Six, stage directions).

Thought: Williams uses music to emphasize the subjective and memory nature of the play.

The music seems to answer his question, while Tom thinks it over. He searches his pockets. (Scene Six stage directions.)

Thought: Williams uses music to emphasize the subjective and memory nature of the play.

"There was a Jim O'Connor we both knew in high school-[then, with effort] If that is the one that Tom is bringing to dinner-you'll have to excuse me, I won't come to the table." (6.30, Laura).

"You remember that wonderful write-up I had in The Torch?"

"Yes!"

"It said I was bound to succeed in anything I went into!" (6.126-6.128, Jim and Laura)

Thought: Jim, just like Amanda, spends excessive time discussing both the glory days of his past and his dreams for the future.

Thought: Just as Amanda, Laura is so haunted by her own past that it debilitates her living in the present.

Laura is still huddled upon the sofa, her feet drawn under her, her head resting on a pale blue pillow, her eyes wide and mysteriously watchful. The new floor lamp with its shade of rose-colored silk gives a soft, becoming light to her face, bringing out the fragile, unearthly prettiness which usually escapes attention. (Scene Seven, stage directions.)

Thought: Williams uses light to emphasize the subjective and memory nature of the play.

"I—don't suppose—you remember me—at all?"

"You know I have an idea I've seen you before. I had that idea soon as you opened the door. It seemed almost like I was about to remember your name. But the name I started to call you—wasn't a name? And so I stopped myself before I said it." (7.75, 7.76, Laura and Jim),

Thought: Although to a lesser degree than her mother, Laura, too, lives in a piece of the past, recalling her feelings for Jim.

"Blue Roses! My gosh, yes—Blue Roses! That's what I had on my tongue when you opened the door! Isn't it funny what tricks memory plays?" (7.78, Jim).

Thought: Jim's line about memory playing tricks has a greater context in the play as a whole – raising the question as to what tricks Tom's memory might be playing on us.

"You modern young people are so much more serious-minded than my generation. I was so gay as a girl!"

"You haven' changed, Mrs. Wingfield."

"Tonight I'm rejuvenated! The gaiety of the occasion, Mr. O'Connor." (7.276-7.278, Amanda and Jim).

Thought: The presence of only a single gentleman caller sent Amanda back to her role as a Southern Belle.

"No, Ma'am, not work but—Betty!"

[He crosses deliberately to pick up his hat. The band at the Paradise Dance Hall goes into a tender waltz.]

"Betty? Betty? Who's—Betty?"

[There is an ominous cracking sound in the sky.] (7.289, 7.290, Jim and Amanda, Scene Seven stage directions).

Thought: Williams uses obvious and dramatic effects in this play on the grounds that memory can dramatize and alter reality. Interestingly enough, just like the characters we are watching, we become ensconced in an alternate reality.

"Then all at once my sister touches my shoulder. I turn around and look into her eyes. Oh, Laura, Laura, I tried to leave you behind me, but I am more faithful than I intended to be! I reach for a cigarette, I cross the street, I run into the movies or a bar, I buy a drink, I speak to the nearest stranger—anything that can blow your candles out! For nowadays the world is lit by lightning! Blow out your candles, Laura—and so, goodbye… (7.321, Tom).

Thought: Although he escapes his family in body, Tom's memory is forever stuck in his past, just as Amanda's.

Weakness Quotes

Laura is seated in the delicate ivory chair at the small clawfoot table. She wears a dress of soft violet material for a kimono – her hair is tied back from her forehead with a ribbon. She is washing and polishing her collection of glass. (Scene Two, stage directions).

Thought: Emphasizing her fragility, Laura is constantly surrounded by delicate and breakable objects, furniture, and clothing.

"'I wonder,' she said, 'If you could be talking about that terribly shy little girl who dropped out of school after only a few days' attendance?'

"And she said, 'No – I remember her perfectly now. Her hands shook so that she couldn't hit the right keys! The first time we gave a speed test, she broke down completely – was sick at the stomach and almost had to be carried into the wash room! After that morning she never showed up anymore. We phoned the house but never got any answer.'" (2.16, Amanda)

Thought: Laura's shy qualities are so extreme as to inhibit normal activity.

"I couldn't go back there. I – threw up – on the floor!" (2.25, Laura).

Thought: Laura uses her shyness to avoid reality and retreat into her own world.

"When I had that attack of pleurosis – he asked me what was the matter when I came back." (2.45, Laura).

Thought: Laura's physical weaknesses and sickness highlight her shyness and mental fragility.

Laura utters a startled, doubtful laugh. She reaches quickly for a piece of glass. (Scene Two, stage directions).

Thought: Laura uses the glass animals as an escape from reality, just as Tom uses the movies.

"But mother—"

"Yes?"

[in a tone of frightened apology]: "I'm crippled!"

"Nonsense, Laura, I've told you never, never to use that word." (2.47-2.50, Laura and Amanda).

Thought: Amanda's later frustration with Laura's shyness stems from her inability to see Laura as having any issues at all.

With an outraged groan he tears the coat off again, splitting the shoulder of it, and hurls it across the room. It strikes against the shelf of Laura's glass collection, and there is a tinkle of shattering glass. Laura cries out as if wounded.

[Music.]

[Screen legend: "The Glass Menagerie."]

"My glass!—menagerie…[She covers her face and turns away.] (Scene Three stage directions, 3.18, Laura)

Thought: The music "The Glass Menagerie" serves to connect Laura's fragility with that of her glass ornaments.

She crosses through the portieres and draws them together behind her. Tom is left with Laura. Laura clings weakly to the mantel with her face averted. Tom stares at her stupidly for a moment. Then he crosses to the shelf. He drops awkwardly on his knees to collect the fallen glass, glancing at Laura as if he would speak but couldn't. (Scene Three, stage directions).

Thought: Unlike Amanda, Tom recognizes much of Laura's fragility, and additionally recognizes it reflected in the glass menagerie.

A second later she cries out. Tom springs up and crosses to the door. Tom opens the door.

"Laura?"

"I'm all right. I slipped, but I'm all right." (Scene Four stage directions, 4.29, 4.30, Tom and Laura).

Thought: Laura's physical weaknesses and sickness highlight her shyness and mental fragility.

"Laura!"

[Legend on screen: "Laura." Music: "The Glass Menagerie."]

"—Oh.—Laura."

"You know how Laura is. So quiet but—still water runs deep! She notices things and I think she—broods about them…A few days ago I came in and she was crying." (4.53, Scene Four stage directions, 4.54, 4.55).

Thought: Although Laura has fragile and weak elements, she is a perceptive character, noticing things about her mother and brother that others miss.

"I mean that as soon as Laura has got somebody to take care of her, married, a home of her own, independent-why, then you'll be free to go wherever you please, on land, on sea, whichever way the wind blows you! But until that time you've got to look out for your sister. I don't say me because I'm old and don't matter! I say for your sister because she's young and dependent." (4.93, Amanda).

Thought: Amanda understands parts of Laura's fragility – her dependence on someone to provide her a home – but misses others, such as her physical weakness and the truly debilitating effect of her shyness.

"I put her in business college—a dismal failure! Frightened so it made her sick at the stomach. I took her over to the Young People's League at the church. Another fiasco. She spoke to nobody, nobody spoke to her. Now all she does is fool with those pieces of glass and play those worn-out records. What kind of life is that for a girl to lead?" (4.93, Amanda).

Thought: Amanda's concern over Laura's fragility is in part based on Laura's failure to meet what Amanda considers social norms.

"Mother, you mustn't expect too much of Laura."

"What do you mean?"

"Laura seems all those things to you and me because she's ours and we love her. We don't even notice she's crippled anymore." (5.120-5.122, Tom and Amanda).

Thought: Tom is more aware of Laura's nature than Amanda.

"Laura is very different from other girls."

[…]

"…in the eyes of others—strangers—she's terribly shy and lives in a world of her own and those things make her seem a little peculiar to people outside the house."

[…]

"She lives in a world of her own—a world of little glass ornaments, Mother…She plays old phonograph records and—that's about all—" (5.126, 5.128, 5.132, Tom).

Thought: Tom understands that Laura uses the glass and the Victrola to escape from the world, but never is able to explicitly connect that he and his sister are doing the same thing.

"I knew that Jim and Laura had known each other at Soldan, and I had heard Laura speak admiringly of his voice. I didn't know if Jim remembered her or not. In high school Laura had been as unobtrusive as Jim had been astonishing." (6.1, Tom).

Thought: Jim presents a character with the opposite of Laura's fragility, which may be why she is so drawn to him.

A fragile, unearthly prettiness has come out in Laura: she is like a piece of translucent glass touched by light, given a momentary radiance, not actual, not lasting. (Stage directions, Scene Six).

Thought: Laura's beauty is inherently tied to her fragility.

"Why are you trembling?"

"Mother, you've made me so nervous!"

"How have I made you nervous?"

"By all this fuss! You make it seem so important!" (6.2-6.5, Amanda and Laura.)

Thought: Laura's shyness puts her constantly at odds with her mother.

"There was a Jim O'Connor we both knew in high school—[then, with effort] If that is the one that Tom is bringing to dinner—you'll have to excuse me, I won't come to the table. (6.30, Laura).

Thought: Despite her shyness and weakness, Laura takes seemingly firm stands against her mother.

"Please, please, please, you go!"

"You'll have to go the door because I can't."

"I can't go either!"

"Why?"

"I'm sick!" (6.51-6.57, Laura and Amanda).

Thought: Laura uses her physical weaknesses to explain her mental ones.

"Excuse me—I haven't finished playing the Victrola…"[She turns awkwardly and hurries into the front room. She pauses a second by the Victrola. Then she catches her breath and darts through the portieres like a frightened deer.] (6.69, Scene Six stage directions).

Thought: Laura uses the Victrola as means to explain retreating, just as Tom uses the movies.

Laura suddenly stumbles; she catches at a chair with a faint moan. (Scene Six stage directions).

Thought: Laura's fragility manifests itself physically.

Laura, stretched out on the sofa, clenches her hand to her lips, to hold back a shuddering sob. (Scene Six stage directions).

Thought: Laura is acutely aware of and bothered by her deficiencies.

Laura sits up nervously as Jim enters. She can hardly speak from the almost intolerable strain of being alone with a stranger. (Scene Seven, stage directions).

Thought: Although she has feelings for Jim, Laura is at first unable to enjoy his company because of her shyness.

"And everybody was seated before I came in. I had to walk in front of all those people. My seat was in the back row. I had to go clumping all the way up the aisle with everyone watching!" (7.103, Laura).

Thought: When Laura finally reveals some stories from high school, we, the audience, begin to understand where her shyness comes from.

She remains by the table, picks up a piece from the glass menagerie collection, and turns it in her hands to cover her tumult. (Scene Seven stage directions.)

Thought: Laura uses the glass menagerie to try to escape from the reality of her current situation with Jim.

"I don't do anything—much. Oh, please don't think I sit around doing nothing! My glass collection takes up a good deal of time. Glass is something you have to take good care of." (7.185, Laura).

Thought: Laura is similar to the glass not only in her fragility, but in her need to be looked after, paid attention to.

"You know what I judge to be the trouble with you? Inferiority complex! Know what that is? That's what they call it when someone low-rates himself. I understand because I had it, too." (7.188, Jim).

Thought: Just like Tom, Jim recognizes Laura's situation. However, unlike Tom, Jim tries to do something about it.

"Little articles of it, they're ornaments, mostly! Most of them are little animals made out of glass, the tiniest little animals in the world. Mother calls them a glass menagerie! Here's an example of one, if you'd like to see it! This one is one of the oldest. It's nearly thirteen…Oh be careful—if you breathe, it breaks!" (7.197, Laura).

Thought: Laura describes not only the fragility of the glass, but emphasizes its size, harking back to the epigraph of the text, "Nobody, not even the rain, has such small hands."

"Oh, but I'd step on you!"

"I'm not made out of glass." (7.225, 7.226, Laura and Jim).

Thought: Jim again appears the opposite of Laura; she is shy and fragile, he is most certainly not.

They suddenly bump into the table, and the glass piece on it falls to the floor. Jim stops the dance. (Scene Seven, stage directions).

Thought: Here we see the danger of bringing glass off the shelf, or Laura out of her secret world: something might break.

"Aw, aw, aw. Is it broken?"

"Now it is just like all the other horses."

"It's lost it's—"

"Horn! It doesn't matter. Maybe it's a blessing in disguise." (7.254-7.257, Jim and Laura).

Thought: When she calls the unicorn breaking a "blessing in disguise," Laura starts to think that being drawn out from her secret world isn't so bad after all.

"I don't have favorites much. It's no tragedy, Freckles. Glass breaks so easily. No matter how careful you are. The traffic jars the shelves and things fall off them." (7.259, Laura).

Thought: Laura recognizes the inevitability of breaking when handling fragile objects – she also recognizes that this applies to her.

"The horn was removed to feel less—freakish! Now he will feel more at home with the other horses, the ones that don't have horns…" (7.261, Laura).

Thought: Laura starts to feel a part of reality, like everyone else, after Jim dances with her.

Tom smashes his glass on the floor. He plunges out on the fire escape, slamming the door. Laura screams in fright. The dance-hall music becomes louder. To stands on the fire escape, gripping the rail. The moon breaks through the storm clouds, illuminating his face. (Scene Seven, stage directions.)

Thought: While Jim is careful and apologizes for the tiniest breaking of the unicorn's horn, Tom smashes glass; Tom is unable to communicate with his sister the way Jim did.

"I would have stopped, but I was always pursued by something. It always came upon me, unawares, taking me altogether by surprise. Perhaps it was a familiar bit of music. Perhaps it was only a piece of transparent glass. Perhaps I am walking along a street at night, in some strange city, before I have found companions. I pass the lighted window of a shop where perfume is sold. The window is filled with pieces of colored glass, tiny transparent bottles in delicate colors, like bits of a shattered rainbow. Then all at one my sister touches my shoulder." (7.321, Tom).

Thought: Laura, despite her apparent weakness and fragility, has an incredibly strong hold on her brother, which lasts over both time and distance.

Deception and Lies Quotes

To begin with, I turn back time. I reverse it to that quaint period, the thirties, where the huge middle class of America was matriculating in a school for the blind. Their eyes had failed them, or they had failed their eyes, and so they were having their fingers pressed forcibly down on the fiery Braille alphabet of a dissolving economy. (1.1, Tom).

Thought: Just as all the members of the Wingfield family have retreated from reality, so, according to Tom, has the rest of the country, choosing to ignore what is going on around them.

I am the narrator of the play, and also a character in it. The other characters are my mother, Amanda, and my sister, Laura, and a gentlemen caller who appears in the final scenes. He is the most realistic character in the play, being an emissary from a world of reality that we were somehow set apart from. But since I have a poet's weakness for symbols, I am using this character as a symbol; he is the long-delayed but always expected something that we live for. (1.1, Tom).

Thought: Tom openly recognizes that Jim is different from the members of the Wingfield family in that he is facing reality, rather than in denial of it.

[lightly] "Temperament like a Metropolitan star!" (1.8, Amanda).

Thought: Amanda fails to recognize that Tom is truly mad at her, treating his snapping comment as a joke.

"Resume your seat, little sister - I want you to stay fresh and pretty - for gentlemen callers!" (1.14, Amanda).

Thought: While Laura's and Tom's retreat from reality is more subtle, Amanda projects self-delusion to a great degree.

"No, dear, you go in front and study your typewriter chart. Or practice your shorthand a little. Stay fresh and pretty! – It's almost time for our gentlemen callers to start arriving. [She flounces girlishly toward the kitchenette] How many do you suppose we're going to entertain this afternoon?" (1.35, Amanda).

Thought: It is because of her obsession with the past that Amanda is so unable to see the present for what it is.

"Not one gentlemen caller? It can't be true! There must be a flood, there must have been a tornado!" (1.37, Amanda).

Thought: Despite repeated attempts that her children make to explain Laura's current situation, Amanda remains blind to the facts.

Laura draws a long breath and gets awkwardly to her feet. She crosses to the Victrola and winds it up. (Scene Two, stage directions).

Thought: Just as Tom uses the movies, Laura uses objects such as the Victrola and her glass menagerie to escape reality.

"I went into the art museum and the bird house at the Zoo. I visited the penguins every day! Sometimes I did without lunch and went to the movies. Lately I've been spending most of my afternoons in the Jewel Box, that big glass house where they raise the tropical flowers." (2.29, Laura).

Thought: Laura retreats into pseudo-worlds to avoid the real one.

"When I had that attack of pleurosis – he asked me what was the matter when I came back. I said pleurosis – he thought that I said Blue Roses! So that's what he always called me after that. Whenever he saw me, he'd holler, 'Hello, Blue Roses!'" (2.45, Laura).

Thought: Laura is drawn to Jim because of his ability to create names and thoughts of an altered reality, such as the ones she chooses to live in.

[in a tone of frightened apology]: "I'm crippled!"

"Nonsense, Laura, I've told you never, never to use that word. Why, you're not crippled, you just have a little defect – hardly noticeable, even! When people have some slight disadvantage like that, they cultivate other things to male up for it – develop charm – and vivacity – and – charm! That's all you have to do!" (2.47-2.50, Laura and Amanda).

Thought: Amanda is blinded by a mother's love to the actualities of Laura's situation.

"Let me tell you—" "I don't want to hear anymore!" (3.20, 3.21, Amanda and Tom).

Thought: Tom chooses to forcibly shut out reality, choosing instead to escape to the movies.

[with great enthusiasm]: "Try and you will succeed! [The notion makes her breathless.] Why, you - you're just full of natural endowments! Both of my children-they're unusual children! Don't you think I know it? I'm so-proud! Happy and-feel I've-so much to be thankful for..." (4.39, Amanda).

Thought: Amanda deludes herself into thinking that matters are far better than they actually are.

"Oh, I can see the handwriting on the wall as plain as I can see the nose in front of my face! It's terrifying! More and more you remind me of your father! He was out all hours without explanation!—Then left! Goodbye! And me with the bag to hold. I saw that letter you got from the Merchant Marine. I know what you're dreaming of. I'm not standing here blindfolded. Very well, then. Then do it! But not till there's somebody to take your place." (4.91, Amanda).

Thought: Ironically, Amanda claims she is not blindfolded, when in fact she is blind to Laura's real predicament and Tom's real needs.

Across the alley from us was the Paradise Dance Hall. On evenings in the spring the windows and doors were open and the music came outdoors. Sometimes the lights were turned out except for a large glass sphere that hung from the ceiling. It would turn rather slowly about and filter the dusk with delicate rainbow colors. Then the orchestra would play a waltz or a tango, something that had a slow and sensuous rhythm. Couples would come outside, to the relative privacy of the alley. You would see them kissing behind ash pits and telephone poles. This was the compensation for lives that passed like mine, without any change or adventure. Adventure and change were imminent this year. They were waiting around the corner for all these kids. Suspended in the mist over Berchtesgaden, caught in the folds of Chamberlain's umbrella. In Spain there was Guernica. But here there was only hot swing music and liquor, dance halls, bars, and movies, and sex that hung in the gloom like a chandelier and flooded the world with brief, deceptive rainbows…All the world was waiting for bombardments! (5.10, Tom).

Thought: Just as Tom escapes to the movies to avoid reality, so, he claims, are all the other members of society.

"A fire escape landing's a poor excuse for a porch." [She spreads a newspaper and sits down, gracefully and demurely as if she were settling into a swing on a Mississippi veranda]. (5.11, Amanda).

Thought: Amanda's body language and motions serve to identify the great magnitude of her self-delusion.

"Laura seems all those things to you and me because she's ours and we love her. We don't even notice she's crippled anymore."

"Don't say crippled! You know I never allow that word to be used!" (5.120-5.122, Tom and Amanda).

Thought: Amanda establishes roles and obligations within her family to help her avoid having to deal with reality.

"Laura is very different from other girls."

[...]

"...in the eyes of others-strangers-she's terribly shy and lives in a world of her own and those things make her seem a little peculiar to people outside the house."

[...]

"She lives in a world of her own-a world of little glass ornaments, Mother...She plays old phonograph records and-that's about all-". (5.126, 5.128, 5.132, Tom)

Thought: Tom fully understands Laura's retreat from reality.

Yes, movies! Look at them-[a wave toward the marvels of Grand Avenue]. All of those glamorous people-having adventures-hogging it all, gobbling the whole thing up! You know what happens? People go to the movies instead of moving! Hollywood characters are supposed to have all the adventures for everybody in America, while everybody in America sits in a dark room and watches them have them! Yes, until there's a war. That's when adventure becomes available to the masses! Everyone's dish, not only Gable's! Then the people in the dark room come out of the dark room to have some adventures themselves-goody, goody! It's our turn now, to go to the South Sea Island-to make a safari-to be exotic, far off! But I'm not patient. I don't want to wait till then. I'm tired of the movies and I am about to move! (6.114, Tom).

Thought: Just as Tom escapes reality by going to the movies, so, he says, does the general population.

At first, before Jim's warmth overcomes her paralyzing shyness, Laura's voice is thin and breathless, as though she had just run up a flight of stairs. Jim's attitude is gently humorous. While the incident is apparently unimportant, it is to Laura the climax of her secret life. (Scene Seven stage directions).

Thought: Jim is so appealing to Laura for his ability to enter her own secret world and interact with her there.

"You don't know things anywhere! You live in a dream; you manufacture illusions!" (7.317, Amanda).

Thought: Ironically, Amanda accuses Tom of manufacturing illusions, not recognizing that she herself is guilty of the same thing.

Dreams, Hopes, and Plans Quotes

I am the narrator of the play, and also a character in it. The other characters are my mother, Amanda, and my sister, Laura, and a gentlemen caller who appears in the final scenes. He is the most realistic character in the play, being an emissary from a world of reality that we were somehow set apart from. But since I have a poet's weakness for symbols, I am using this character as a symbol; he is the long-delayed but always expected something that we live for. (1.1, Tom).

Thought: Tom understands that Jim is more than just a gentleman caller; he is the epitome of everything Amanda desires for her daughter.

"What are we going to do, what is going to become of us, what is the future?" (2.10, Amanda).

Thought: Amanda oscillates between reminiscing over the past and planning for the future.

"Oh! I felt so weak I could barely keep on my feet! I had to sit down while they got me a glass of water! Fifty dollars' tuition, all of our plans – my hopes and ambitions for you – just gone up the spout, just gone up the spout like that." (2.16, Amanda).

Thought: Amanda's plans for her children's futures fail because they are irreconcilable with what her children actually want.

"So what are we going to do the rest of our lives? Stay home and watch the parades go by? Amuse ourselves with the glass menagerie, darling? Eternally play those worn-out phonograph records your father left as a painful reminder of him? We won't have a business career – we've given that up because it gave us nervous indigestion! [She laughs wearily.] What is there left but dependency all our lives? I know so well what becomes of unmarried woman who aren't prepared to occupy a position. I've seen such pitiful cases in the South – barely tolerated spinsters living upon the grudging patronage of sister's husband or brother's wife! – stuck away in some little mousetrap of a room – encouraged by one in-law to visit another – little birdlike women without any nest – eating the crust of humility all their life!

Is that the future that we've mapped out for ourselves? I swear it's the only alternative I can think of! [She pauses.] It isn't a very pleasant alternative, is it? [She pauses again.] Of course – some girls do marry." (2.34, Amanda).

Thought: Amanda's attempts to have Laura marry are based on a fear of the future, not on any intrinsic value of love.

"An evening at home rarely passed without some illusion to this image, this specter, this hope...Even when he wasn't mentioned, his presence hung in Mother's preoccupied look and in my sister's frightened, apologetic manner – hung like a sentence passed upon the Wingfields!" (3.1, Tom).

Thought: The language Tom uses to describe the gentleman caller is reminiscent of the effect on the audience of the hanging portrait – thus, the gentleman is for the future what Tom's father is for the past.

[screen legend: "Plans and Provisions."]

"We have to be making some plans and provisions for her. She's older than you, two years, and nothing has happened. She just drifts along doing nothing. It frightens me terribly how she just drifts along." (Scene Four stage directions, 4.87, Amanda).

Thought: Amanda's concern over the future always revolves around her children, not herself.

"Down at the warehouse, aren't there-nice young men?" (4.97, Amanda).

Thought: Amanda places on Tom not only the burden of supporting the family in the present, but also of taking care of its future.

"I'll tell you what I wished for on the moon. Success and happiness for my precious children! I wish for that whenever there's a moon, and when there isn't a moon, I wish for it, too." (5.23, Amanda).

Thought: Amanda chastises Tom for being a 'selfish dreamer,' yet her own dreams for the future are even less attainable.

"Yes, but Mr. O'Connor is not a family man."

"He might be, mightn't he? Some time in the future?"

"I see. Plans and provisions." (5.92-5.54. Tom and Amanda).

Thought: Amanda draws elaborate plans for the future, even including a man she has never met.

"You are the only young man I know of who ignores the fact that the future becomes present, the present past, and the past turns into everlasting regret if you don't plan for it!" (5.95, Amanda).

Thought: Although Amanda discloses nuggets of perspective on the progression of time, she herself spends all of her time oscillating between the past and the future.

"Then he has visions of being advanced in the world! Any young man who studies public speaking is aiming to have an executive job some day! And radio engineering? A thing for the future! Both of these facts are very illuminating. Those are the sort of things that a mother should know concerning any young man who comes to call on her daughter. Seriously or—not." (5.117, Amanda).

Thought: Amanda makes grand claims about the future using very little fact or evidence from the present.

"What shall I wish for, Mother?"

[her voice trembling and her eyes suddenly filling with tears]: "Happiness! Good fortune!" (5.140, 5.141, Laura, Amanda).

Thought: Amanda chastises Tom for being a 'selfish dreamer,' yet her own dreams take on a dream-like and superstitious quality almost foolish in nature.

"But sister is all by her lonesome. You go keep her company in the parlor! I'll give you this lovely old candelabrum that used to be on the altar at the Church of the Heavenly Rest." (7.34, Amanda).

Thought: Amanda shamelessly takes action towards her plan for she and Laura's future.

"Well, it was quite a wonderful exposition. What impressed me most was the Hall of Science. Gives you an idea of what the future will be in America, even more wonderful than the present time is!" (7.67, Jim).

Thought: Jim's idealism toward the future reflects the American Dream of progress and growth.

"You think of yourself as having the only problems, as being the only one who is disappointed. But just look around you and you will see lots of people as disappointed as you are. For instance, I hoped when I was going to high school that I would be further along this time, six years later, than I am now." (7.76, Jim).

Thought: Jim, like Amanda, discusses the past, but in a more instructive and beneficial way.

"My signature isn't worth very much right now. But some day—maybe—it will increase in value! Being disappointed is one thing and being discouraged is something else. I am disappointed but I am not discouraged." (7.158, Jim).

Thought: Jim's idealism toward the future reflects the American Dream of progress and growth.

"Because I believe in the future of television! I wish to be ready to go up right along with it. Therefore I'm planning to get in on the ground floor. In fact I've already made the right connections and all that remains is for the industry itself to get under way! Full steam...Knowledge—Zzzzzp! Money—Zzzzzzp!—Power! That's the cycle democracy is built on!" (7.192, Jim).

Thought: Jim's idealism toward the future reflects the American Dream of progress and growth.

"Well, now that you've found your way, I want you to be a very frequent caller! Not just occasional but all the time. Oh, we're going to have a lot of gay times together! I see them coming!" (7.282, Amanda).

Thought: Amanda's character is made more tragic by her unfounded optimism.

"GO, then! Go to the moon-you selfish dreamer!" (7.320, Amanda).

Thought: While she chastises Tom for being a dreamer, Amanda doesn't recognize that her own plans for the future have become mere dreams.

Abandonment Quotes

"A blown-up photograph of the father hangs on the wall of the living room, to the left of the archway. It is the face of a very handsome young man in a doughboy's First World War cap. He is gallantly smiling, ineluctably smiling, as if to say "I will be smiling forever." (stage directions, Scene One).

Thought: Tom's father seems to show no regret at having abandoned his family.

There is a fifth character in the play who doesn't appear except in this larger-than-life-size photograph over the mantel. This is our father who left us a long time ago. He was a telephone man who fell in love with long distances; he gave up his job with the telephone company and skipped the light fantastic out of town…

The last we heard of him was a picture postcard from Mazatlan, on the Pacific coast of Mexico, containing a message of two words: "Hello - Goodbye!" and no address. (1.1, Tom).

Thought: Tom's desire to leave the Wingfield apartment originally emulates that of his father. Yet, later, unlike is father, Tom is not able to make a clean break.

"Listen! You think I'm crazy about the warehouse? [He bends fiercely toward her slight figure.] You think I'm in love with Continental Shoemakers? You think that I want to spend fifty-five years down there in that - celotex interior! with-fluorescent-tubes! Look! I'd rather somebody packed up a crowbar and battered out my brains-than go back mornings! I go! Every time you come in yelling that Goddamn 'Rise and Shine! Rise and Shine!' I say to myself, 'How lucky dead people are!' But I get up. I go! For sixty-five dollars a month I give up all that I dream of doing and being ever! And you say self-self's all I ever think of! Why, listen, if self is what I thought of, Mother, I'd be where he is-GONE! [He points to his father's picture.] As far as the system of transportation reaches!" (3.34, Tom).

Thought: Tom makes it clear that the only reason he has not left home is that he does not value the self over the family enough to abandon his mom and sister.

"And, oh, I forgot! There was a big stage show! The headliner on this stage show was Malvolio the Magician…But the wonderfullest trick of all was the coffin trick. We nailed him into a coffin and hr got out of the coffin without removing one nail. There is trick that would come in handy for me-get me out of this two-by-four situation!

…"You know it don't take much intelligence to get yourself into a nailed-up coffin, Laura. But who the hell ever got himself out of one without removing one nail?"

As if in answer, the father's grinning photograph lights up. (4.9, 4.13, Tom, Scene Four stage directions).

Thought: It seems that when Tom's father abandoned the Wingfield family, there was little or no effect on the remaining remembers.

"We have to do all that we can to build ourselves up. In these trying times we live in, all that we have to cling to is-each other…" (4.31, Amanda).

Thought: Tom's eventual abandonment of his family is made more tragic by Amanda's comments that they need each other.

"However, you do act strangely. I-I'm not criticizing, understand that! I know your ambitions do not lie in the warehouse, that like everybody in the whole wide world-you've had to-make sacrifices, but-Tom-Tom-life's not easy, it calls for-Spartan endurance! There's so many things in my heart that I cannot describe to you! I've never told you but I-loved your father…"

[gentle]: "I know that, Mother." (4.61, 4.62, Amanda and Tom).

Thought: Amanda's character is made more sympathetic by her discussions of the husband that abandoned her.

"And you-when I see you taking after his ways! Staying out late-and-well, you had been drinking the night you were in that-terrifying condition! Laura says that you hate the apartment and that you go out nights to get away from it! Is that true, Tom?" (4.63, Amanda).

Thought: Amanda accurately points out that Tom takes after his father, both in his nights out and in his later abandonment of the family.

"Oh, I can see the handwriting on the wall as plain as I can see the nose in front of my face! It's terrifying! More and more you remind me of your father! He was out all hours without explanation!-Then left! Goodbye! And me with the bag to hold. I saw that letter you got from the Merchant Marine. I know what you're dreaming of. I'm not standing here blindfolded. Very well, then. Then do it! But not till there's somebody to take your place." (4.91, Amanda).

Thought: Amanda is OK with the idea of Tom abandoning the family – as long as there is someone around to take care of Laura.

"How about your mother?"

"I'm like my father. The bastard son of a bastard! Did you notice how he's grinning in his picture in there? And he's been absent going in sixteen years!" (6.127, 6.128, Jim and Tom).

Thought: Tom preferentially sides with his missing father rather than his mother.

"I married a man who worked for a telephone company! That gallantly smiling man over there! A telephone man who-fell in love with long distance! Now he travels and I don't even know where!" (6.139, Amanda).

Thought: Amanda's character is made more sympathetic by her discussions of the husband that abandoned her.

"That's right, now that you've had us all make such fools of ourselves. The effort, the preparations, all the expense! The new floor lamp, the rug, the clothes for Laura! All for what? To entertain some other girl's fiancé! Go to the movies, go! Don't think about us, an unmarried sister who's crippled and has no job! Don't let anything interfere with your selfish pleasure! Just go, go, go-to the movies!" (7.319, Amanda).

Thought: Amanda believes that Tom abandoned the family – in spirit – by bringing an unsuitable caller home for Laura.

"GO, then! Go to the moon-you selfish dreamer!" (7.320, Amanda).

Thought: Amanda finally gives up on Tom, in a way abandoning him before he abandons her and Laura.

"I didn't go to the moon - I went much further-for time is the longest distance between two poles. Not long after that I was fired for writing a poem on the lid of a shoe-box. I left St. Louis. I descended the steps of this fire escape for a last time and followed, from then on, in my father's footsteps, attempting to find in motion what was lost in space." (7.321, Tom).

Thought: Before confessing that his abandonment was not successful, Tom suggests that his leaving was similar to his father's.

"Then all at once my sister touches my shoulder. I turn around and look into her eyes. Oh, Laura, Laura, I tried to leave you behind me, but I am more faithful than I intended to be! I reach for a cigarette, I cross the street, I run into the movies or a bar, I buy a drink, I speak to the nearest anything-anything that can blow your candles out! For nowadays the world is lit by lightning! Blow out your candles, Laura-and so, goodbye… (7.321, Tom).

Thought: Although he tried to abandon his family, Tom could not abandon his sister, Laura, in spirit.

Marriage Quotes

"A blown-up photograph of the father hangs on the wall of the living room, to the left of the archway. It is the face of a very handsome young man in a doughboy's First World War cap. He is gallantly smiling, ineluctably smiling, as if to say "I will be smiling forever." (stage directions, Scene One).

Thought: Amanda's figure is made more sympathetic because her husband abandoned her.

There is a fifth character in the play who doesn't appear except in this larger-than-life-size photograph over the mantel. This is our father who left us a long time ago. He was a telephone man who fell in love with long distances; he gave up his job with the telephone company and skipped the light fantastic out of town…

The last we heard of him was a picture postcard from Mazatlan, on the Pacific coast of Mexico, containing a message of two words: "Hello - Goodbye!" and no address. (1.1, Tom).

Thought: Tom's father displayed no regret as to his failed marriage with Amanda.

"There was young Champ Laughlin who later became vice president of the Delta Planters Bank. Hadley Stevenson who was drowned in Moon Lake and left his widow one hundred and fifty thousand in government bonds. There were the Cutrere brothers, Wesley and Bates. Bates was one of my bright particular beaux! He got in a quarrel with that wild Wainwright boy. They shot it out on the floor of Moon Lake Casino. Bates was shot through the stomach. Died in the ambulance on his way to Memphis. His widow was also well provided-for, came into eight or ten thousand acres, that's all. She married him on the rebound – never loved her – carried my picture on him the night he died! And there was that boy that every girl in the Delta had set her cap for! That beautiful, brilliant young Fitzhugh boy from Green County!" (1.29, Amanda).

Thought: Amanda's lengthy description of other marriages hints at a sadness as to her own failed marriage.

"That Fitzhugh boy went North and made a fortune – came to be known as the Wolf of Wall Street! He has the Midas touch, whatever he touched turned to gold! And I could have been Mrs. Duncan J. Fitzhugh, mind you! But – I picked your father!" (1.33, Amanda).

Thought: Amanda sees her other potential marriages as lost opportunities.

"Mother's afraid I'm going to be an old maid." (1.38, Laura).

Thought: Laura recognizes clearly which life goals her mother has assigned to her.

"I know so well what becomes of unmarried woman who aren't prepared to occupy a position. I've seen such pitiful cases in the South - barely tolerated spinsters living upon the grudging patronage of sister's husband or brother's wife! - stuck away in some little mousetrap of a room - encouraged by one in-law to visit another - little birdlike women without any nest - eating the crust of humility all their life!

Is that the future that we've mapped out for ourselves? I swear it's the only alternative I can think of! [She pauses.] It isn't a very pleasant alternative, is it? [She pauses again.] Of course - some girls do marry." (2.34, Amanda).

Thought: Just as she believes it is the duty of the man to bring home money, Amanda thinks it is Laura's duty to marry.

"I didn't care for the girl that he went out with. Emily Meisenbach. Emily was the best-dressed girl at Soldan. She never struck me, though, as being sincere…It says in the Personal Section – they're engaged. That's – six years ago! They must be married by now." (2.45, Laura).

Thought: Laura subtly envies what she thinks is another woman's marriage to Jim.

"Girls that aren't cut out for business careers usually wind up married to some nice man. [She gets up with a spark of revival.] Sister, that's what you'll do!" (2.46, Amanda.)

Thought: Amanda sees marriage as a tool for Laura's safety and security.

"When people have some slight disadvantage like that, they cultivate other things to male up for it - develop charm - and vivacity - and - charm! That's all you have to do!" [She turns again to the photograph]. "One thing your father always had plenty of – was charm!" (2.50, Amanda).

Thought: Despite his having left her, Amanda's comments with regard to her husband are all attempts at being positive.

"After the fiasco at Rubicam's Business college, the idea of getting a gentlemen caller for Laura began to play a more important part in mother's calculations. It became an obsession. Like some archetype of the universal unconscious, the image of the gentleman caller haunted our small apartment…" (3.1, Tom).

Thought: Just as Tom pursues escape, an ultimately unobtainable goal, so Amanda pursues what is eventually unobtainable as well: a husband for Laura.

Now we see Amanda; her hair is in metal curlers and she is wearing a very old bathrobe, much too large for her slight figure, a relic of the faithless Mr. Wingfield. (Scene Three, stage directions).

Thought: Amanda's failed marriage is ever-present throughout the play, adding to her desperation to find a husband for Laura.

"There's so many things in my heart that I cannot describe to you! I've never told you but I—loved your father…"

[gentle]: "I know that, Mother." (4.61, 4.62, Amanda and Tom).

Thought: For Amanda, marriage is not necessarily associated with love.

"I guess she's the type that people call home girls."

"There's no such type, and if there is, it's a pity! That is unless the home is hers, with a husband." (4.88, 4.99, Tom and Amanda).

Thought: Amanda thinks about marriage and gender roles in very traditional ways.

"I mean that as soon as Laura has got somebody to take care of her, married, a home of her own, independent—why, then you'll be free to go wherever you please, on land, on sea, whichever way the wind blows you! But until that time you've got to look out for your sister. I don't say me because I'm old and don't matter! I say for your sister because she's young and dependent." (4.93, Amanda).

Thought: Amanda sees a husband for Laura as a replacement for the role Tom currently plays.

"Down at the warehouse, aren't there—nice young men?" (4.97, Amanda).

Thought: Amanda places on Tom the responsibility to find Laura a husband.

"Lots of fellows meet girls whom they don't marry!"

"Oh, talk sensibly, Tom—and don't be sarcastic!" (5.82, 5.83).

Thought: Amanda uses older and more traditional ideas on dating and marriage, in contrast to Tom.

"That is the way such things are handled to keep a young woman from making a tragic mistake!"

"Then how did you happen to make a tragic mistake?"

"That innocent look of your father's has everyone fooled! He smiled—the world was enchanted! No girl can do worse than put herself at the mercy of a handsome appearance! I hope that Mr. O'Connor is not too good-looking." (5.101-5.103).

Thought: Amanda has very specific requirements for Laura's potential husband, many of them deriving from the quirks of her own marriage.

"All of my gentlemen callers were sons of planters and so of course I assumed that I would be married to one and raise my family on a large piece of lad with plenty of servants. But man proposes—and woman accepts the proposal! To vary that old, old saying a little bit—I married no planter! I married a man who worked for a telephone company! That gallantly smiling man over there! A telephone man who—fell in love with long distance! Now he travels and I don't even know where!" (6.139, Amanda).

Thought: Even in the presence of guests, Amanda can not stop from discussing her absent husband.

"It said in the 'Personal' section that you were—engaged!"

"I know, but I wasn't impressed by that—propaganda!"

"It wasn't—the truth?"

"Only in Emily's optimistic opinion!" (7.171-7.174).

Thought: *The Glass Menagerie* presents marriage as an institution pursued primarily by women.

Gender Quotes

"Resume your seat, little sister – I want you to stay fresh and pretty – for gentlemen callers!" (1.14, Amanda).

Thought: Amanda believes in the importance of a woman's appearance.

"One Sunday afternoon in Blue Mountain – your mother received – seventeen! – gentlemen callers! Why, sometimes there weren't enough chairs to accommodate them all. We had to send the nigger over to bring in folding chairs from the parish house." (1.21, Amanda).

Thought: Amanda judges a woman's worth by how much attention she receives from men.

Image on screen, Amanda as a girl on a porch, greeting callers. (Stage directions, Scene One).

Thought: Amanda's character is largely defined by her former attractiveness to men.

"They knew how to entertain their gentlemen callers. It wasn't enough for a girl to be possessed of a pretty face and a graceful figure – although I wasn't slighted in either respect. She also needed to have a nimble wit and a tongue to meet all occasions." (1.27, Amanda).

Thought: Amanda assigns certain responsibilities to her daughter and her son, according to their genders.

"No, dear, you go in front and study your typewriter chart. Or practice your shorthand a little. Stay fresh and pretty! - It's almost time for our gentlemen callers to start arriving. [She flounces girlishly toward the kitchenette] How many do you suppose we're going to entertain this afternoon?" (1.35, Amanda).

Thought: Amanda's repeated instructions to 'stay fresh and pretty' underscore the value she places on attractiveness for women.

"Mother's afraid I'm going to be an old maid." (1.38, Laura).

Thought: Laura recognizes clearly the gender roles she is expected to fill, and her mother's fears that she may fail to do so.

"I know so well what becomes of unmarried woman who aren't prepared to occupy a position. I've seen such pitiful cases in the South - barely tolerated spinsters living upon the grudging patronage of sister's husband or brother's wife! - stuck away in some little mousetrap of a room - encouraged by one in-law to visit another - little birdlike women without any nest - eating the crust of humility all their life!

Is that the future that we've mapped out for ourselves? I swear it's the only alternative I can think of! [She pauses.] It isn't a very pleasant alternative, is it? [She pauses again.] Of course - some girls do marry." (2.34, Amanda).

Thought: Amanda uses the gender roles of her own time to prescribe certain goals and desires for her daughter.

"Girls that aren't cut out for business careers usually wind up married to some nice man. [She gets up with a spark of revival.] Sister, that's what you'll do!" (2.46, Amanda.)

Thought: Amanda gets her thoughts on gender roles from observing the outside world.

"...she conducted a vigorous campaign on the telephone, roping in the subscribers to one of those magazines for matrons called The Homemaker's Companion, the type of journal that features the serialized sublimations of ladies of letters who think in terms of delicate cuplike breasts, slim, tapering waists, rich, creamy thighs, eyes like wood smoke in autumn, fingers that soothe and caress like strains of music, bodies as powerful as Etruscan sculpture." (3.1, Tom).

Thought: Amanda's work is rooted in the same gender roles that fuel her goals for her daughter.

"I guess she's the type that people call home girls."

"There's no such type, and if there is, it's a pity! That is unless the home is hers, with a husband." (4.88, 4.99, Tom and Amanda).

Thought: Amanda rates a woman's worth by her marital status. Interestingly enough, she never addresses where this leaves her herself.

"I mean that as soon as Laura has got somebody to take care of her, married, a home of her own, independent-why, then you'll be free to go wherever you please, on land, on sea, whichever way the wind blows you! But until that time you've got to look out for your sister. I don't say me because I'm old and don't matter! I say for your sister because she's young and dependent." (4.93, Amanda).

Thought: Because of gender stereotyping, Amanda makes it Tom's responsibility to look out for his older sister Laura.

"I put her in business college-a dismal failure! Frightened so it made her sick at the stomach. I took her over to the Young People's League at the church. Another fiasco. She spoke to nobody, nobody spoke to her. Now all she does is fool with those pieces of glass and play those worn-out records. What kind of life is that for a girl to lead?" (4.93, Amanda).

Thought: Amanda's plans for Laura are based not on a desire for her daughter's own satisfaction, but a fulfillment of the gender roles she sees in the world around her.

"Do you realize he's the first young man we've introduced to your sister? It's terrible, disgraceful that poor little sister has never received a single gentleman caller!" (5. 61, Amanda).

Thought: Amanda places the responsibility on Tom to help Laura fulfill the duties of her gender.

"Character's what to look for in a man." (5.107, Amanda).

Thought: While Amanda values looks for women, she does not for men.

"However, he'll know about Laura when he gets here. When he sees how lovely and sweet and pretty she is, he'll thank his lucky stars he was asked to dinner." (5.119, Amanda).

Thought: While Amanda inquires as to Jim's character and job, she still sees Laura's appeal as being in her looks.

Amanda produces two powder puffs which she wraps in handkerchiefs and stuffs in Laura's bosom. (Scene Six, stage directions).

Thought: While Jim will later recognize Laura for her individuality, Amanda tries to make her into a cookie-cutter woman.

"You make it seem like we were setting a trap."

"All pretty girls are a trap, a pretty trap, and men expect them to be."

Legend on screen: "A Pretty Trap." (6.14, 6.15, Laura and Amanda, Scene Six stage directions).

Thought: Amanda believes in using looks, not personality, to attract men.

"Now look at yourself, young lady. This is the prettiest you will ever be!" (6.15, Amanda).

Thought: Amanda takes pride in physical appearance over all else.

"It's rare for a girl as sweet an' pretty as Laura to be domestic! But Laura is, thank heavens, not only pretty but also very domestic." (6.139, Amanda).

Thought: Amanda exaggerates and fabricates qualities to make her daughter seem more attractive.

"Look how big my shadow is when I stretch!" (7.214, Jim).

Thought: While Laura doesn't fit the gender roles prescribed to her, Jim fits a typical masculine role.

Love Quotes

"I know so well what becomes of unmarried woman who aren't prepared to occupy a position. I've seen such pitiful cases in the South - barely tolerated spinsters living upon the grudging patronage of sister's husband or brother's wife! - stuck away in some little mousetrap of a room - encouraged by one in-law to visit another - little birdlike women without any nest - eating the crust of humility all their life!

Is that the future that we've mapped out for ourselves? I swear it's the only alternative I can think of! [She pauses.] It isn't a very pleasant alternative, is it? [She pauses again.] Of course - some girls do marry." (2.34, Amanda).

Thought: Amanda makes no mention of love in her discussion of marriage for Laura.

"Haven't you ever liked some boy?"

"Yes. I liked one once. I came across his picture a while ago." (2.34, 2.35, Amanda and Laura).

Thought: The strength of Laura's feelings for Jim is at first unclear.

"He used to call me – Blue Roses."

Screen image: Blue Roses. (2.43, Scene Two stage directions).

Thought: Laura's feelings for Jim stem from his ability to recognize her as someone unique from others.

There's so many things in my heart that I cannot describe to you! I've never told you but I-loved your father…"

[gentle]: "I know that, Mother." (4.61, 4.62, Amanda and Tom).

Thought: Amanda does not automatically associate love with marriage.

"Laura, Laura, were you in love with that boy?"

"I don't know, Mother. All I know is I couldn't sit at the table if it was him!" (6.35, 6.36, Amanda and Laura).

Thought: The intensity of Laura's feelings for Jim becomes evident as the play progresses.

"Ha-ha, that's very funny! [Suddenly he is serious.] I'm glad to see that you have a sense of humor. You know –you're—well—very different! Surprisingly different from anyone else I know! [His voice becomes soft and hesitant with a genuine feeling.] Do you mind me telling you that? I mean it in a nice way—You make me feel sort of—I don't know how to put it! I'm usually pretty good at expressing things, but—this is something that I don't know how to say! Has anyone ever told you that you were pretty? Well, you are! In a very different way from anyone else. And all the nicer because of the difference, too." (7.262, Jim).

Thought: Jim's feelings for Laura are based on her as an individual, not her prescribed gender role.

"I wish that you were my sister. I'd teach you to have some confidence in yourself. The different people are not like other people, but being different is nothing to be ashamed of. Because other people are not such wonderful people. They're one hundred times one thousand. You're one times one! They walk all over the earth. You just stay here. They're common as—weeds,

but—you—well, you're—Blue Roses!" (7.262, Jim).

Thought: While Amanda discusses jonquils endlessly, the flower associated with Laura is original and an appropriate fit for her unique character.

"In all respects—believe me! Your eyes—your hair—are pretty! Your hands are pretty! [He catches hold of her hand.] You think I'm making this up because I'm invited to dinner and have to be nice. Oh, I could do that! I could put on an act for you, Laura, and say lots of things without being very sincere. But this time I am. I'm talking to you sincerely. I happen to notice you had this inferiority complex that keeps you from feeling comfortable with people. Somebody needs to build your confidence up ad make you proud instead of shy and turning away and—blushing. Somebody—ought to—kiss you, Laura!" (7.266, Jim).

Thought: Jim's feelings for Laura have much to do with his desire to help her, to save her from her world of retreat and solitude.

His hand slips slowly up her arm to her shoulder as the music swells tumultuously. He suddenly turns her about and kisses her on the lips. When he releases her, Laura sinks on the sofa with a bright, dazed look. Jim backs away and fishes in his pocket for a cigarette…

…Laura slowly raises and opens her hand. It still contains the little broken glass animal. She looks at it with a tender, bewildered expression. (Scene Seven, stage directions.)

Thought: Laura's fragility is heightened by the intensity of her feelings for Jim.

"No, Laura, I can't. As I was just explaining, I've—got strings on me. Laura, I've—been going steady! I go out all the time with a girl named Betty. She's a home-girl like you, and Catholic, and Irish, and in a great many ways we—get along fine. I met her last summer on a moonlight boat trip up the river to Alton, on the Majestic. Well—right away from the start it was—love!"

[Legend: Love!] (7.268, Jim, Scene Seven stage directions).

Thought: Although Jim claims to be in love with Betty, his description that they 'get along fine' hardly holds a candle to the emotions for Laura that he described.

"Being in love has made a new man of me! The power of love is really pretty tremendous! Love is something that—changes the whole world, Laura!" (7.268, Jim).

Thought: Jim is unaware of the detrimental effect of his words on Laura.

Drugs and Alcohol Quotes

"I think you've been doing things that you're ashamed of. That's why you act like this. I don't believe that you go every night to the movies. Nobody goes to the movies night after night. Nobody in their right minds goes to the movies as often as you pretend to. People don't go to the movies at nearly midnight, and movies don't let out at two A.M. Come in stumbling. Muttering to yourself like a maniac! You get three hours' sleep and then go to work. Oh, I can picture the way you're doing down there. Moping, doping, because you're in no condition." (3.31, Amanda).

Thought: Amanda combines all her fears of bad behavior into her singular fear that Tom will be a man who drinks.

Tom appears at the top of the alley. After each solemn boom of the bell tower, he shakes a little noisemaker or rattle as if to express the tiny spasm of man in contrast to the sustained power and dignity of the Almighty. This and the unsteadiness of his advance make it evident that he has been drinking. As he climbs the few steps to the fire escape landing light steals up inside. Laura appears in the front room in a nightdress. She notices that Tom's bed is empty. Tom fishes in his pockets for his door key, removing a motley assortment of articles in the search, including a shower of movie ticket stubs and an empty bottle. (Scene Four, stage directions).

Thought: Williams uses props to display both that Tom is in fact drinking and that he also was telling the truth about going to the movies.

[with great enthusiasm]: "Try and you will succeed! [The notion makes her breathless.] Why, you - you're just full of natural endowments! Both of my children-they're unusual children! Don't you think I know it? I'm so-proud! Happy and-feel I've-so much to be thankful for but—promise me one thing, son!"

"What, Mother?"

"Promise, son, you'll—never be a drunkard!"

[turns to her grinning]: "I will never be a drunkard, Mother."

"That's what frightened me so, that you'd be drinking!" (4.39-4.43, Amanda and Tom).

Thought: Just as Amanda ignored the problems of the present by focusing on the past, she similarly blinds herself to Tom's biggest problems by focusing instead on an absurd fear of alcoholism.

"Find out one that's clean-living—doesn't drink and ask him out for sister!" (4.101, Amanda).

Thought: Amanda's concern for alcoholism is excessive, extending both to her son and to her daughter's potential suitor.

"Tom, he—doesn't drink?"

"Why do you ask me that?"

"Your father did!"

"Don't get started on that!"

"He does drink, then?"

"Not that I know of!"

"Make sure, be certain! The last thing I want for my daughter's a boy who drinks!" (5.71-5.77, Amanda and Tom).

Thought: Only towards the end of the play does Williams reveal the source of Amanda's concern over alcohol: that her husband drank.

"Old maids are better off than wives of drunkards!" (5.77, Amanda).

Thought: Amanda's fear of alcoholism is so great that she even compromises her desire for Laura to get married at any cost.

"Irish on both sides! Gracious! And doesn't drink?"

"Shall I call him up and ask him right this minute?"

"The only way to find out about those things is to make discreet inquiries at the proper moment. When I was a girl in Blue Mountain and it was suspected that a young man drank, the girl whose attentions he had been receiving, if ay girl was, would sometimes speak to the minister of his church, or rather her father would if her father was living, and sort of feel him out on the young man's character. That is the way such things are discreetly handled to keep a young woman from making a tragic mistake. (5. 99-5.101, Amanda and Tom).

Thought: Amanda's views on alcohol, much like the rest of her views, derive from a different time period and are slightly outdated.

Plot Analysis

Classic Plot Analysis

Initial Situation

Laura is painfully shy, Amanda lives in the past, Tom hates his life, and they have no father.
Wow, things completely suck to start off. As with many initial situations, we get the idea that things have been going on like this for a long time – Tom's been going to the movies and getting scolded for it, Laura's been allowing her shyness to run her life, and Amanda's been narrating about her past as if everyone in the world cared as much about jonquils as she did.

Conflict

Amanda insists that Laura must get married; Tom hates his life and wants to leave.
Now we have this end goal to shoot for – find Laura a husband. The conflict part, or the why-is-this-difficult part, has to do with Laura's shyness and fragility. We wonder if, in this rough process, she will break like a piece of glass. Oh, and then there's Tom's conflict, both with his mother and with the life he is leading at the moment.

Complication

Tom gets a gentlemen caller for Laura, but it turns out to be the Jim from her past.
Yes, that does complicate things. Especially since Laura is ridiculously shy with normal people and inhumanly shy with high school heroes she used to be infatuated with.

Climax

The gentleman caller connects with Laura, kisses her, breaks the horn off her glass unicorn.
How did we know this was the climax? Well, Williams does call it "the climax of her secret life," with the 'her' being Laura. That's sort of a tip off. Also, this is what we've been building towards the whole time – we knew the gentleman caller had to come at some point, and we knew with all this fragile glass all over the place that sooner or later something was going to break.

Suspense

Jim turns out to be engaged; Amanda yells at Tom.
Just when we thought things were going well. We feel suspense here because there's this panicky sort of "Oh no! What do we do now?!" Except not "we" so much as Amanda and Laura.

Denouement

Tom reveals to us rather anticlimactically that he leaves his family shortly after.
This is 'falling action' because it doesn't give you that sense of building towards something. We're backing away from the big dramatic scenes of yelling and kissing and breaking and instead are looking at the aftermath.

Conclusion

Although he separated himself from his family physically, Tom reveals that he was always

haunted by the memory of the sister.

Time to wrap things up. Or, in this case, time for narrator Tom to reveal he was never really able to wrap things up. This conclusion sort of messes with us, because we thought once Tom left the family that would be it. But now we realize our big final end point doesn't really have such a note of finality to it.

Booker's Seven Basic Plots Analysis: Tragedy

Anticipation Stage
Amanda commits to finding a gentleman caller for Laura.
Amanda feels that her family is unfulfilled, so she focuses her energies on finding a husband for Laura. She anticipates Laura getting married sometime in the near future.

Dream Stage
Tom gets a gentleman caller for Laura.
Tom and Amanda commit to the course of action, roping in this Jim character to act as the gentleman caller. The dream, much like the anticipation, is that Laura will get married.

Frustration Stage
Laura is being difficult because the gentleman caller is a figure from her past.
Amanda is extremely frustrated with Laura's fragility, shyness, and general refusal to interact with Jim. Amanda becomes more forceful, yelling at her daughter and demanding that she open the door for the guest.

Nightmare Stage
Jim turns out to be engaged.
Amanda is left with no control over the situation here. The dream spirals into nightmare as we realize that Laura can't possibly marry this guy.

Destruction or Death Wish Stage
Tom ends his role in the family.
Tom doesn't really die, but you could say that he fulfills a metaphorical death wish with respect to his role as family provider.

Three Act Plot Analysis

Act I
A gentleman caller is needed; Laura is shy; Tom wants to leave the family.

Act II
A gentleman caller comes; Laura stops being shy; Tom hints he is about to leave the family.

Act III
The gentleman caller is engaged to be married and leaves; Laura retreats back to shyness;

Tom abandons his family.

Study Questions

1. How is "The American Dream" presented here, and what comments are made on it? Is it an unrealistic dream? Detrimental?
2. How does Williams's "plastic theatre" – that is, the exaggerated music at key moments, the obvious lighting tactics, the over-dramatized nature of, well, the drama – support the content of the play? Is this a good play to use "plastic theatre" techniques for?
3. How does the epigraph comment on Laura or the overall themes of the play?
4. With all this denial flying about the place, what are these three characters hiding from each other? What do they try to conceal from the audience, even? From themselves? How do their interactions with each other cause friction with respect to their hidden demons?
5. How does it work to have Tom both narrating the action and participating in the action? Do you trust him as a narrator? Does it change the way you see the play?

Characters

All Characters

Laura Wingfield Character Analysis

Laura is oh-so-fragile, not unlike her glass collection. Hey! Coincidence? Probably not. In fact, definitely not. Laura parallels her glass collection in a few different ways. To begin, she has the same sort of translucent beauty, the same delicate exterior. She is also very breakable, in the sense that she freaks out at the slightest social challenge and runs away. What's cool is that these two things are connected – the beauty and the fragility – and complement each other. A piece of glass is very beautiful because it is so breakable. Right? And Williams uses the tinkly music that he calls "The Glass Menagerie" in order to connect them. There's also her slightly crippled leg, a physical manifestation of this fragility.

Like her mother and brother, Laura retreats from reality. She's so far departed that she can't even see reality anymore. She spends her days going to the zoo, or polishing her glass, or playing records. She has no social interaction, and even her brother, Tom, who clearly cares for her, doesn't really break into her little world. Until Jim. Laura opens up to Jim in a way that she hasn't done with anyone else. He recognizes that she is unique – that's where this Blue Roses business fits in. Have YOU ever seen a blue rose? Exactly. Jim recognizes that Laura is one-in-a-million. While Laura's mother tries to conform her to some standard of Southern

femininity, Jim appreciates her for who she is. And she loves him for it.

Which brings us to Tom and Laura. Laura ends up mediating between her mother and brother, asking him to apologize, trying to prevent a confrontation when Tom comes home drunk. Laura's pretty much a why-can't-we-all-get-along girl. But she's also perceptive; Laura understands Tom's desire to escape and explains it to her mother. She understands that Amanda relishes her stories of the past and makes that clear to Tom. This perceptiveness, along with her dependence on Tom, her break-ability, and her innocence, all add up to one guilt-inducing memory for the older Tom, the narrator.

Laura Wingfield Timeline and Summary

- Laura has a tension-filled dinner with Tom and Amanda.
- She remarks that her mother thinks she will be an old maid.
- Laura polishes her glass collection but then pretends to have been typing when her mother approaches.
- When confronted, she admits to having dropped out of her typing class.
- She discusses her shyness and crippled leg and plays the Victrola obsessively.
- She discusses Jim, whom she had a thing for in high school, and his nickname for her, "Blue Roses."
- She sits demurely on the stage getting bathed in light while the others talk.
- Laura flips out when Tom accidentally breaks some of her glass animals.
- Laura hangs out with a drunken Tom and they discuss his movie-going experience.
- She encourages Tom to apologize to their mother.
- She goes out on the fire escape with her mother who wishes on the moon.
- Laura is forced to get dressed up in preparation for the gentleman caller.
- She discovers that the Jim coming to visit is the same one she used to fawn over at pep rallies.
- Laura refuses to answer the door.
- Laura answers the door and then runs away to the Victrola.
- She spends dinner lying out on the couch.
- She and Jim discuss high school, her crippled leg or lack thereof, and his demigod status.
- She discloses that she dropped out of high school.
- Laura asks about Jim's old girlfriend.
- Laura shows Jim the unicorn, her favorite piece of glass.
- She dances with Jim and they break the horn off of the unicorn; she believes it to be "a blessing in disguise."
- She is kissed by Jim.
- Laura finds out Jim is engaged and gives him the unicorn as a "souvenir."
- She is comforted, silently, by her mother, while Tom gives his closing speech.
- Right on cue with Tom's line about candles, Laura blows the candles out.

Tom Wingfield Character Analysis

Tom's your narrator. You can tell because he introduces himself that way and then proceeds to, well, narrate the play. He waxes poetic a lot about the nature of memory, the 1930s, glass, and actually things in general. He just likes to wax poetic. But Tom focuses on what ends up being the core of his character, his desire to get the hell out of town. Tom wants adventure, excitement, new experiences, new places; in short, the opposite of what he was getting working at the warehouse and living at home. He is also a reader and a writer, yet chastised by his mother for the former and eventually fired for the latter. Tom describes his current situation as imprisonment, and his frequent forays onto the fire "escape" are just about as coincidental as Laura similarity to her glass collection. He also uses the movies to briefly experience vicariously what he longs to have in his own life. So the question is...does he escape?

Tom reveals at the end of the play that he could never shake off the memory of Laura. He seems to feel guilty at having left her behind; but he never says anything about his mother! Which brings up the whole topic of Tom's interaction with these women. Although he doesn't seem to understand the nature of her secret world the way Jim does, Tom at least recognizes that Laura has a secret world to begin with. And he clearly cares very deeply for her, struck with guilt and self-loathing when he breaks her glass animals with his coat. Amanda, on the other hand, he's not so chummy with. In fact, he calls her a witch at one point. You could even say she's the one to really drive him away.

There's also the issue of the missing father. Tom frequently comments on the fact that he is similar to his father – willing to abandon the family and never come back. He almost seems to use this as an excuse, a sort of it's-in-my-genes kind of thing when he tells his plan to Jim. Whether or not Tom can be criticized on moral grounds for abandoning the family is open to debate. And we're all ears.

Tom Wingfield Timeline and Summary

- Tom introduces himself as the narrator and explains the memory nature of the play.
- He gives the background info about his father having left them.
- He fights with his mother at the table.
- Tom hangs out on the fire escape and discusses his mother's desire for his sister to be a house wife.
- Tom argues with Amanda about his reading Lawrence and going to the movies.
- He waxes poetic about his desire to leave and/or be dead rather than work in a shoe factory.
- Tom delivers a sarcastic tirade about the evil things he does when he claims to be at the movies.
- Tom hurls his coat in anger and accidentally breaks some of the glass animals.
- He comes home drunk and bumps into Laura, telling her all about his movie-going experiences.
- Tom discusses the notion of escaping from a coffin.

- Tom apologizes to his mother on Laura's request.
- Tom dreams about adventure – out loud, to his mother.
- He talks about the dreamy Paradise Dance Hall across the street.
- Tom reveals to Amanda that he got a gentleman caller for Laura.
- Tom goes to the movies...again.
- He smokes on the fire escape and talks about Jim
- He shows up with Jim and talks to him about adventure.
- Tom confesses that he did not pay the light bill.
- He endures dinner with Amanda and Jim.
- He finds out Jim is engaged from Amanda and gets yelled at for it.
- Tom takes off for the movies.
- Narrator Tom gives his closing speech and reveals that he left his family shortly after that night, seeking adventure and other non-boring activities.
- Tom makes it clear that he always felt guilty about leaving Laura, and couldn't get her out of his mind.

Amanda Wingfield Character Analysis

Oh, Amanda – where do we begin? What's that song? Something about some woman stuck in 1985. Yeah – that's pretty much Amanda, except it's the early 1900's. Because the present is so depressing, what with her unmarried daughter, moody son, and then that whole U.S. Depression-era thing, Amanda chooses to live in the past. This is her retreat from reality, though it takes a different form than Laura's or Tom's.

But it's not all about the past. Amanda also looks into the future, making what she calls "plans and provisions," single-mindedly for her children. In fact, as annoying as all the nagging about keeping one's elbows off the table is, Amanda is actually a very loving mother. Other than shooting the breeze about when she used to have gentlemen callers in her youth, Amanda doesn't really think too much about herself. Her mothering is extreme, to say the least, all-encompassing, and, for Tom, suffocating to some degree.

Which makes us wonder about that missing husband of hers. Although Amanda doesn't seem to attach much emotional value to marriage (she sees it as a tool for her daughter to be supported by a man), she confesses to Tom that she did loved his father. In fact, she spends a lot of her stage directions just looking at his portrait. You sort of have to read between the lines on this one, because Amanda never explicitly tells us much about the guy. You know he peaced out, that he had no regrets (because he smiles all the time), that he was good-looking, charming, and liked his alcohol. But Amanda is pretty controlled about the whole thing, chattering on about him abandoning her as though it doesn't hurt, when clearly, for a woman of Southern tradition, being left by her husband is a pretty awful ordeal. She shows considerable strength – which you might alternatively call denial – in dealing with the situation.

We would love to blame Amanda for her ridiculously stereotyped projections of gender roles, and the way she forces certain plans of the future onto her children. But, honestly – the woman

has a point. They do need a plan. Tom does need to support them or they starve. And as for the gender roles – she was raised in the South in the early 1900s, so what are you going to do?

Amanda Wingfield Timeline and Summary

- Amanda fights with Tom at the dinner table
- She recalls her glory days as a young Southern Belle and wishes Laura had gentlemen callers.
- She is upset at Laura for having dropped out of her typing class.
- Amanda distresses about being on the poor side of things.
- She denies that Laura is crippled and daydreams about her missing husband's charm.
- She makes humiliating phone calls trying to sell magazine subscriptions.
- Amanda argues with Tom about his reading Lawrence and going to the movies.
- She accuses him of not actually going to the movies, but participating in drinking and other debauchery.
- Amanda refuses to speak to Tom over breakfast.
- She asks Tom to find a gentleman caller for Laura, one that doesn't drink.
- She calls Tom selfish.
- Amanda makes some more humiliating magazine subscription phone calls.
- She is super excited to find that Tom got a gentleman caller for Laura and obsesses about the appearance of the house.
- She calls Laura out to the fire escape to wish on the moon.
- Amanda gets all dolled up for the gentleman caller.
- Amanda stuffs Laura's shirt with powder puffs.
- Amanda insists that Laura answer the door.
- She acts all Southern Belle-ish around the two boys and makes them say grace at dinner.
- She sends Jim out to the living room to see Laura.
- Amanda dreams (aloud) about the great times they will all have together.
- She finds out Jim is engaged.
- She yells at Tom.
- Amanda comforts Laura while Tom gives an ending speech.

Jim O'Connor Character Analysis

Jim is ordinary. Seem simplistic? That's what we thought, too, when we read the introduction and Williams only says "a nice, ordinary, young man." Not too much to work with, right? WRONG! Maybe old Williams missed it, but we think there's more to Jim than being ordinary. Like what, you might ask? Read on, skeptical friend.

First of all, Jim is the only character to break through into Laura's secret world. That's pretty impressive. But what makes him so special, anyway? Well he's pretty much the most sincere person in the play. He's very honest, friendly, chipper – the man has freckles, for heaven's

sake. He's completely trustworthy and, as such, we the audience get to trust him. Which is cool because, since Tom is the one telling the story, everything he says is a little biased; after all, he's probably trying to convince us he's not a total jerk at the end of the play. But back to Jim again.

We were totally in Jim's corner until the whole engaged thing. Who goes around kissing girls when they're engaged? It is interesting, though, the attitude that Jim takes towards the whole situation. At first we thought he was hitting on Laura, but then he kept talking about her self-confidence, and at one point says that he wishes she were *his* sister. Which means (hopefully) that his interest in her isn't actually sexual or even romantic in nature. You know, aside from the kissing. Jim simply has an honest desire to help. But at the same time, he's obviously very drawn to Laura – and yes, in a romantic sense. He admits this to her, poetically describing her beauty, how she makes him feel different than any other girl. And then he tries – and fails – to talk about his love for his fiancé. In discussing Betty, Jim is forced to resort to abstracts and exclamations, suggesting that what he has with Betty isn't love at all. Poor Jim – such a nice, ordinary, young man.

Jim O'Connor Timeline and Summary

- Jim shows up at the Wingfield apartment with Tom and greets Laura when she answers the door.
- Jim chills out on the fire escape with Tom and discusses his ambitious plans for his public speaking future.
- He has dinner with Amanda and Tom.
- He goes out to see Laura in the living room.
- He and Laura discuss high school, her crippled leg or lack thereof, and his demigod status.
- He signs Laura's program.
- Jim says he's not with his ex-girlfriend anymore.
- Jim discusses his plans for the future and tells Laura to have more confidence.
- He makes Laura dance with him and breaks the horn off of her unicorn.
- He hits on Laura and kisses her.
- Then he remembers he has a fiancée and talks about how in love with her he is.
- He reveals to Amanda that he is engaged.
- Jim leaves.

Character Roles

The fact is, you can make an argument for any one of several different protagonists in *The Glass Menagerie*. Don't believe us? Fine! Here we go...

Protagonist
Tom
It totally makes sense that Tom is the protagonist because he's the one telling the story and the

narrator is almost always the protagonist. We get his thoughts and we see his character sympathetically.

Protagonist
Amanda
The protagonist has to be Amanda because in the classic plot of a tragedy, she fulfills the role of committing to a dream and then having that dream completely squashed.

Protagonist
Laura
Doubtlessly, the protagonist is Laura. She's the only one that, we, the audience, don't get annoyed with all the time or feel the need to judge on the basis of his/her awful moral decisions, and she has all these great protagonist qualities like being perceptive and kind and beautiful. She even has the fatal flaw built in, what with the shyness and all.

Antagonist
Amanda
Amanda is only the antagonist if you think that Tom is the protagonist. Even then, she's more a pain in his side than that a villain. But we'll make the argument anyway. Amanda harasses and badgers Tom into being unhappy and restless. She begrudges him small pleasures like drinking and going to the movies, and she insults him for wanting to be happy himself instead of looking out for his family. The question is, does this make Amanda merely a concerned mother, or is she a legitimate antagonist?

Foil
Jim to Tom
Jim has a lot of characteristics that Tom doesn't. Naturally, Amanda loves the guy. When Jim comes to visit, it's like when that over-achieving friend comes over and your parents are all like, "Why can't you be more like him?" But getting to the specifics: Tom is a sloth lacking ambition, according to his mother, whereas Jim has dreams of making it big. Tom goes to the movies, whereas Jim takes public speaking lessons. They seem quite different, yet they both end up, in one way or another, screwing over Amanda and Laura. Neither lives up to the inflated roles Amanda creates for them, which may say more about Amanda and her absurd dreams than it does about either man.

Character Clues

Direct Characterization
Yep, that's right. Williams is a member of the "let's just spell it out" camp. To be fair, this depends on whether you're reading the play or seeing it up on the stage. If you're reading it, there are short character descriptions in the beginning that tell you how to interpret each character. But even if you're only seeing it on the stage, Williams helps you out. Tom pretty much blatantly tells Amanda (and therefore the audience) what had previously been subtext about Laura: "Laura is very different…she's terribly shy and lives in a world of her own…a world of little glass ornaments."

Habits

As you might have noticed, Laura constantly lives in a world of little glass ornaments. Her habit reflects her character, since retreating from reality means she is ill-equipped to handle others socially, and the whole glass thing means she's fragile, as we've already discussed at length. Then there's Tom, whose habit of going to the movies signifies his need to escape from reality. Hmm…this whole escape thing is looking like a family habit.

Family Life

Because this is a family drama, the characters are characterized by their relations to the others in their family. Laura is subordinate to her mother; therefore, she is passive in nature. Amanda is controlling of her children's lives and frantic about their futures; therefore, she seeks to control the future since she's freaking out about the present. Jim refuses at times to talk to his mother; therefore, he escapes reality at times by simply ignoring that it's there. Got it?

Speech and Dialogue

Southern Accent, Amanda

Notice how Amanda starts talking differently when Jim comes over? She speaks in a Southern accent ("light food an' light clothes are what warm weather calls fo'"), which, up until that point, we hadn't really heard come out of her mouth. That's because she's reverting to the past, or 'rejuvenated' as she tells Jim.

Pedantic Prose vs. Regular Language, Narrator Tom and Character

So narrator Tom tends to speak in language like, "They were having their fingers pressed forcibly down on the fiery Braille alphabet of a dissolving economy," and the Tom interacting with the other characters reads lines like, "How about—supper?" Now, partly you could say that's because character Tom is talking to other people, and when you're talking to other people you don't expound on your ideas in flowery language because they would look at you funny or whack you over the head. And then you would be partly right. But it also helps us, along with some other tools, discern which Tom is speaking.

Literary Devices

Symbols, Imagery, Allegory

Blue Roses and Jonquils

Yes, we've got some flower stuff going on here. Amanda always talks about jonquils when referring to her past, when she herself was a pretty little Southern Belle surrounded by dozens of gentlemen callers. Jonquils are a type of Narcissus, which is named of course from Greek Mythology and has to do with vanity, or narcissism. Interesting. Also, and we may be getting totally out of hand here, but jonquils are the same thing that we Americans call daffodils, and e.e. cummings, who is referenced to already twice in the play, wrote a poem about daffodils that also discusses roses. Not that that means anything. Back to business: for Amanda, the flowers are reminiscent of the past and signify what she wants for her daughter.

So Laura counters with blue roses. Jim's old nickname for Laura, "Blue Roses," comes to represent Laura's unique and individual self, a self that Jim and only Jim recognizes. Blue roses have this sort of mythical significance of being mysterious, or impossible to come by, which makes sense when you look at Jim's description of Laura as a one-in-a-million girl.

The Glass Menagerie, in particular the Unicorn

The Glass Menagerie is fragile and delicate, just as Laura. This fragility is manifested physically in the glass; as Laura says, "If you breathe, it breaks!" Yowzah. It's also really beautiful, as those of you with unhealthy glass animal fetishes may have already known. Laura has the same kind of beauty – the translucent, other-worldly, delicate kind.

Then there's this unicorn business. When Laura talks about the unicorn, she reveals that it is her favorite glass animal, that it is unique from all the other horses because of its horn. Not that Laura has a horn, as far as we know, but she is really different from most girls, as Jim recognizes. Part of what separates her from the pack is her off-the-charts shyness. So when Jim makes her dance with him, and the horn breaks off the unicorn, Laura calls it a "blessing in disguise" – she is being made to be a normal person. However, when Jim turns out to be engaged, she gives him the unicorn, in a tragic sort of "look what you broke in me" kind of way.

The Movies, The Fire Escape

Tom hates his life and he uses movies, dancing, and the occasional bottle of booze to get him through. Notice how he always heads to the movies when things at home get unbearable, like his mother yelling at him?

And of course, the fire escape. We mean, the fire ESCAPE. Tom keeps hanging out there, partly because of the smoking thing, but really because of the ESCAPE thing. This is foreshadowing. Tom almost escapes…almost escapes…very nearly escapes…and then ESCAPES! Only not really, because he can never truly escape the memory of Laura.

Alcohol

You might have noticed that Amanda has this issue with alcohol. She refuses to let Tom drink, she needs to ensure that Jim doesn't, and she mentions briefly that her irresponsible husband used to. What's cool about this, and why we decided to put it in this oh-so-exclusive section, is that when Amanda talks about alcohol, she isn't just talking about alcohol. She sort of uses it to mean everything bad – like reading D.H. Lawrence and going to the movies and having dreams of adventure. Alcohol also ends up being a connection between Tom and his father: they both drink. Amanda doesn't like Tom "taking after his ways," and we, the wise and perceptive audience, know this means that Tom will, like his father, eventually abandon the family as well.

Setting

The Wingfield apartment in St. Louis.

Tennessee Williams makes a big deal out of telling us all about the apartment. He wants us to

know how the buildings are all stacked up like a beehive, so we get the sense of dehumanization and confinement to working roles. Because the action ONLY takes place at the apartment, we can sense Tom's feelings of being trapped, the fact that he is contained in only one location along with his family. The fire escape, of course, is crucial, being a means of escape and all. It kind of hangs out there like a constant foreshadowing of Tom's eventual escape. It's also, fittingly, the place where narrator Tom does a good deal of his narrating. This makes sense – narrator Tom has already escaped, so he speaks to us from outside the apartment.

Narrator Point of View

First Person (Central Narrator)
The narrator is an older Tom, some years after the scenes that are played out. He defines the way in which the play is presented here, as a "memory scene." Not only does the narrator guide us through the action with, you know, narration, but he also infuses the play with its tone and memory-like appearance. Because we hear the story from the guy in the story, we know it has been altered and adjusted. The point of view, then, becomes hugely important when we consider that objectivity, and potentially accuracy as well, have been removed from this story.

Genre

Family Drama; Tragedy
We say 'tragedy' because things don't really work out so well in the end. Family drama, well, that's pretty self-explanatory, what with the family and the drama and all.

Tone

Melancholy, Reflective, Meta-fictional
The tone of this play is the product of its narrator. Because Tom tells us about the play by looking back from a rather sad state, the scenes are necessarily imbued with narrator Tom's emotions. He regrets having abandoned Laura, so all the scenes are filled with a sense of regret. As for the metafictional stuff, we mean the dramatic music at key moments, the screen projecting images, the general way that we the audience are never allowed to forget that we are watching a play. There's also Tom's introductory speech, where he make reference to the play you are about to see. That's meta-fiction, or, in this case, meta-drama.

Writing Style

Grandiose, pretentious

We thought we would let a quote do the talking here. Here we go:

"Tom appears at the top of the alley. After each solemn boom of the bell in the tower, he shakes a little noisemaker or rattle as if to express the tiny spasm of man in contrast to the sustained power and dignity of the Almighty."

See what we mean about grandiose pretentiousness?

What's Up With the Title?

The Glass Menagerie is a collection of small glass animals that Laura Wingfield obsesses over. She spends her time polishing and, well, obsessing, using the menagerie as a retreat from the real world. The importance of the glass lies in the way Laura mirrors its delicate beauty and fragility.

What's Up With the Epigraph?

"Nobody, not even the rain, has such small hands."
– e. e. cummings

The epigraph comes from an e.e. cummings poem, "somewhere i have never traveled, gladly beyond." What's up with it? Well, small hands sounds like delicate, feminine…sounds like fragile, sounds like…glass! And Laura.

Did You Know?

Trivia

- Tennessee Williams wrote an essay called "The Catastrophe of Success" after *The Glass Menagerie* made him famous, basically saying he hated himself for becoming one of the pampered elite and offering advice to those other poor souls who might someday become rich, famous, and free of care.
- Blue roses served Williams's purpose because they are supposed to be rare or impossible things. But then geneticists came in and ruined it all by manipulating a rose to turn it blue. Why are we telling you this? We have no idea. But they're the coolest roses we've ever seen.
- This play is actually a little bit autobiographical. Or a lot bit. Williams had a sister, a lot like Laura, named Rose. Whoa. He most likely felt guilty about her having a prefrontal lobotomy in St. Louis. Not to mention he, like Tom, had dreams of becoming a writer.

- You know the screen device we kept talking about in the summary? Well, Tennessee invented that idea on the grounds that "each scene contains a particular point (or several)...which is structurally the most important...[which] may be obscured from the audience...This may not be the fault of the play so much as a lack of attention in the audience." And directors' responses to this claim? Most of them found it pretentious and downright annoying, choosing to leave it out of their production.

Steaminess Rating

PG-13
Sex in the glass menagerie...Hmm...Well, there isn't exactly any explicit banging up there on the stage, but things get pretty smokin' hot between Laura and Jim. In fact, we believe Williams calls it "the climax of her secret life." Anyway, she's been harping over this guy for years, and now suddenly he shows up at her house, tells her she's attractive, dances with her, and kisses her, with much staring-into-the-eyes tossed in between. That's about as sexy as Williams lets it get, but we still think it deserves some general parental guidance.

Allusions and Cultural References

Literature, Philosophy, and Mythology
D.H. Lawrence (Scene Three, dialogue line 16)
Shakespeare: Tom's nickname is Shakespeare, *Romeo and Juliet* (Scene Seven, dialogue 296)
e.e. cummings: "somewhere i have never traveled" (epigraph), "The Hours Rise Up Putting Off Stars And It Is" (Scene Six, stage directions)

Best of the Web

Movie or TV Productions
1950 Movie
http://www.imdb.com/title/tt0042509/
This version of *The Glass Menagerie* took some liberties with Tennessee Williams's original script.

1973 Movie
http://www.imdb.com/title/tt0070115/
A film version of *The Glass Menagerie* with Katharine Hepburn as Amanda.

1987 Movie
http://www.imdb.com/title/tt0093093/
This film adaptation of the play was directed by Paul Newman and stars John Malkovich as Tom.

Images
Stage Set-up
http://www.theatredesign.org.uk/despix/dien3.jpg
One production's interpretation of the Wingfield home.

Another Stage Set-up
http://www.colonytheatre.org/shows/ShowPhotos/theGlassMenagerie.jpg
Welcome to the Wingfield living room.

Playbill
http://www.courttheatre.org/home/plays/0506/glass/images/home.jpg
A modern playbill for *The Glass Menagerie*

An Older Playbill
http://www.rosscare.net/Images/The%20Glass%20Menagerie.jpg
This playbill has pictures of the four main characters.

Playbill
http://www.footlightsgallery.com/imagelg/menagerie3.jpg
This one features Christian Slater and Jessica Lange.

Tennessee Williams
http://www.gatewayno.com/images/Williams2.jpg
Here's the man himself, writing.

Documents
"somewhere i have never traveled, gladly beyond"
http://www.poets.org/viewmedia.php/prmMID/15401
Check out the full e.e. cummings poem that the epigraph comes from.

"in time of daffodils"
http://www.americanpoems.com/poets/eecummings/11926
Now check out the poem we were talking about with the daffodils and jonquils in it.

Made in the USA
Lexington, KY
04 December 2014